Social Media Pie

Social Media Pie

How to Enjoy a Bigger Slice of LinkedIn

By

BRENDA MELLER

1st Printing, 2021

ISBN: 978-1-947345-22-5 (print)
ISBN: 978-1-947345-23-2 (digital)

Meller, Brenda
Social Media Pie
Printed in the United States of America
Cover design by Dawn Lewandowski
Book layout and design by Slaven Kovačević
Editing by Jackie Rapetti and Karen Lasater
Indexing by Sophie Bradshaw
Author photograph by Scott Lawrence scottlawrencephoto.com
Makeup by tiffanyeliemakeup.com

Praise for Brenda Meller and Social Media Pie

"There are many ways to indulge in "Social Media Pie", but Brenda's tips and tricks on how to create and get the best results make this a must read for anyone who uses the platform."
~ Tina Marie Wohlfield,
Chief People Strategist at TIMAWO LLC and Author; "STOP, COLLABORATE, and LISTEN"
www.linkedin.com/in/tina-marie-wohlfield-sphr-shrm-scp

You should read Social Media Pie because it makes the torrent of information manageable. Social Media Pie will give you the tools to be effective on LinkedIn in a fun and entertaining manner.
~ Christopher G. Johnson,
Speaker / Trainer and IT Communications Strategist
www.linkedin.com/in/cgjohnson

"There are a lot of "experts" on LinkedIn. What makes Brenda different is Social Media Pie: her approach to shining the spotlight on others, graciously offering LinkedIn strategy tips, and her never-ending quest to helping others create and evolve their personal brand on LinkedIn. Read this book and you'll gain new insights to help propel your results using LinkedIn."
~ Diane Darling, #LinkedInROCKSTARS member, Consultant, and Author; "The Networking Survival Guide, Networking for Career Success" and Curator; "She Said It."
www.linkedin.com/in/dianedarling

"Social Media Pie is a great book for every entrepreneur, small business, or creative individual to have at their fingertips as we all are six degrees separated and this will get you to one degree. It offers a fantastic way to stay connected professionally and find the professionals that have crossed your path from bygone years. PLUS: the tips provide a good way to 'boost' your business and get online visibility."

~ Denise Kulak,
Business Manager at Green Mountain Technologies, Inc.
www.linkedin.com/in/denisegrzechkulak

Brenda Meller's book, Social Media Pie, ignites your appetite for her amazing LinkedIn tips and tricks to pile onto your plate. You won't just want second helpings -- you'll want thirds and fourths. Plus, grab a slice (or in this case buy a copy) for someone else! This book is a guaranteed delicious delight for anyone looking to further develop their presence on LinkedIn.

~ Shawna Ramsey,
Senior Account Director at Merkle
www.linkedin.com/in/shawna01

Brenda is one of those rare breeds that digs in deep on a topic not only for her benefit but for the benefit of those she serves. What I love about her: she serves everyone who follows her. She shares great tips and practical advice on how to make better use of LinkedIn WHILE encouraging us to be better stewards of connections. She is also one of the few people here who will not only teach you how to use this site, she will do it for you.

~ Terry Bean,
Vice President - POP - People Opportunities Promotions
at PKIG | Phil Klein Insurance Group
www.linkedin.com/in/terrybean

Brenda Meller truly helps you to unlock the power of LinkedIn! Her guidance and coaching have positively transformed both my personal and business presence on LinkedIn.

~ Kareem George,
Principal at Culture Traveler
www.linkedin.com/in/kareemgeorge

Brenda has been working with our organization and me personally, for a couple of months. In that short time, she has help us "up our game" in the world of LinkedIn and using that platform to increase our visibility. She has an amazing knowledge of LinkedIn. Tapping into her expertise in refining our profiles, maximizing content and promoting our brand has already begun to produce results.

~ Suzy Alberts,
Employee Benefits Strategist / Account Director
at Comprehensive Benefits, Inc.
www.linkedin.com/in/suzyalberts

Brenda has turned her knowledge of career search, her expertise with LinkedIn, and her genuine Passion for helping people in transition into a web-rich Platform and a Business. Eager job-seekers come to her webinar sessions on rave referrals from others. In these sessions, they are energized and informed about things such as personal branding and how to make their profiles more attention-grabbing. Brenda makes it sound like a piece of cake! No wait, it's pie and coffee--that's part of her Personal Brand!

~ Joe Gritton,
Project Manager
www.linkedin.com/in/joe-gritton

Brenda Meller is a cut above all the other LinkedIn consultants out there. She's a very intuitive teacher and delivers a barrage of whammo LinkedIn tips that are sure to get results. Stop fooling around on social media and start using LinkedIn on purpose; hire Brenda Meller to train your sales team.

~ Michael Angelo Caruso,
Author, Speaker, Online Speaking Coach
www.linkedin.com/in/michaelangelocaruso

Brenda is "ninja-level" at giving specific action steps to take marketing on LinkedIn to the next level. Her concrete "point and click" strategies can make an immediate impact on helping any business leverage the power of LinkedIn (plus, you will love the enthusiasm she has in delivering the information)!! If you haven't yet, connect with her today!

~ Renee Hribar,
Speaker, Trainer, Coach at Renee Hribar International, LLC
www.linkedin.com/in/reneehribar

We hired Brenda to educate our organization on how to optimize LinkedIn for brand awareness and demand generation. We were impressed by Brenda's knowledge and ability to customize content towards our specific organizational needs. The webinar was engaging and practical; many tips provided could be done quickly and easily and we saw an immediate increase with our metrics. In six months, new followers of our company page increased by 35% and we have tripled our monthly engagement statistics. I would highly recommend Meller Marketing and the LinkedIn Optimization webinar format to improve company engagement and brand awareness via the LinkedIn channel.

~ Lora Wilson,
Vice President of Marketing at Zywave
www.linkedin.com/in/lorawilson1

Brenda Meller is one of the most talented individuals for whom I have the pleasure of knowing and working with across a variety of experiences. She has a deep commitment to ensuring the growth and development of the people she encounters. I have found her expertise and insights to be on target with individual and marketing needs and she has a social media savvy that goes beyond just knowing how to make it happen, she knows how to help others make it happen through social media. She brings an unwavering patience to tasks in which collective wisdom is essential to its success, and stays focused on the outcomes that make a positive difference for individuals and organizations.

~ Lee Meadows, PhD,
Author, Speaker, Leadership Consultant
at Meadows Consulting
www.linkedin.com/in/meadowslee

Brenda is remarkable. She was tracking professionals in her LinkedIn training space and keeping tabs on follower totals when she hit upon the idea of publishing her tracking data. In an instant 'Brenda Meller's LinkedIn Rockstars' became a thing. She is marketing savvy, LinkedIn sophisticated and one of the nicest people you'll ever meet. She knows her stuff and is highly respected in our industry.

~ Andy Foote,
#LinkedInROCKSTARS member and Advanced LinkedIn
Strategies Coach at LINKEDINSIGHTS.COM
www.linkedin.com/in/andyfoote

Brenda has provided high quality LinkedIn consulting to our team for several years. She is a true subject matter expert. We have found her to be an excellent coach and trainer. She works very well with our people and presents relevant information concisely and clearly. Brenda is the best. I strongly recommend her if you are looking for resources to assist in improving your use of LinkedIn.
~ Mark Bealin,
Managing Director; Practice Leader Resource Solutions Group
at UHY Advisors
www.linkedin.com/in/markdbealin

Brenda is a *delight* to work with! Attending her LinkedIn training was one of the best, most valuable trainings I've ever had. There's rarely a day when I DON'T use one of Brenda's tips in some form or fashion.
~ Eric McCahill,
Digital Marketing Strategist & Account Executive
www.linkedin.com/in/ericmccahill

I would like to say thank you, Brenda, and acknowledge what a pleasure it has been to work with you as my LinkedIn Coach;-) I'm so proud of my LinkedIn profile after you updated it and really showcased the exciting work that I do. Now when people say, "I'm going to look you up on Linkedin," I feel a sense of gratitude and relief because I know they will see the best of me because of the work you have done.
~Cathy Mott,
Leadership Coach/Author/Speaker/Consultant & Trainer at
CWC Leadership Development, LLC
www.linkedin.com/in/cathy-mottmi

Brenda has delivered individual and group LinkedIn training and content to Detroit Economic Club members over the last couple of years. DEC members consistently give Brenda outstanding ratings and frequently comment how many immediate takeaways they receive. Besides, anyone who is a pie freak like Brenda can't be all bad!

~ Steve Grigorian,
President & CEO at Detroit Economic Club
www.linkedin.com/in/stevegrigorian

We had Brenda conduct her "How to Optimize LinkedIn to Support Your Brand & Generate Leads" for our entire staff – from admins to the CEO, ranging from heavy-users to never-users – and she blew us away! She took the time to help those that needed it, but kept things moving for those keeping up. Many of the suggestions she had, I would never have thought of. After using Brenda's advice, I have seen a dramatic improvement in my LinkedIn engagement.

~Jeff Laskowski,
Senior Manager, Communications
at Original Equipment Suppliers Association
www.linkedin.com/in/laskowskijeff

After my LinkedIn session with Brenda, I realized three things: 1) I need to use LinkedIn more than I do, 2) it's the little things that create big results, and 3) know how you create value for people. When you don't know what you don't know go to somebody who does and Brenda delivers.

~ Scott Wyckoff,
Student Outreach Coordinator/Advisor
www.linkedin.com/in/scottwyckoff

I recently recruited Brenda to speak at Domotex USA, a floor covering trade show. I was responsible for the educational content of the show, and Brenda did me proud! I was able to sit in on her LinkedIn training and learned several things that I did not know. She was thoroughly engaging, energetic, knowledgeable and a great communicator and teacher. I would hire Brenda again for a seminar and strongly recommend her to you! She is a delight!

~ Paul Friederichsen,
Marketing Consultant
www.linkedin.com/in/paulfriederichsen

Table of Contents

Section 7: Miscellaneous & Conclusion

Section 1:

Welcome & Overview

Chapter 1:

Introduction

"In all my work, I try to say - 'You may be given a load of sour lemons, why not try to make a dozen lemon meringue pies?'"

~ Maya Angelou

First things first: I've started each chapter with a famous quote about pies. And I've ended each chapter with some of my LinkedIn connections' favorite pies. I hope you enjoy these!

I've also included LinkedIn URLs for anyone I have mentioned, to make it easier for you to grow your LinkedIn network. But remember to include a personal note and tell them you read their name in this book.

Welcome to my book written especially for YOU. Yes, *you*. Before we get started, I should let you in on a few assumptions I'm making:

1. **You are already on LinkedIn**. I've seen other books out there offering step-by-step instructions for every single area of LinkedIn. This book does not. While we'll go over some basics, this is not a LinkedIn 101. Rather, this book is meant to show you how to get the most out of LinkedIn.

2. **LinkedIn is going to keep changing, again and again.** Even though the network is always evolving, the principles I cover in this book remain true no matter the changes. When writing of a feature that I think may change in the future, I've made note of the date it was written. I also didn't include any screen captures because the platform is continually changing. If you're reading the printed version of this book, you'll also have access to the free digital version which will be updated to reflect changes as needed.

3. **You are open to learning and doing.** One thing I know for certain based on my experience in training thousands of LinkedIn members is this: YOU WILL NOT GAIN ANYTHING FROM THIS BOOK UNLESS YOU TAKE ACTION.

   Also, based on my years of experience training sales teams on LinkedIn: YOUR TEAM WILL NOT IMPROVE THEIR LINKEDIN SUCCESS IF THEY DON'T BELIEVE LINKEDIN IS A USEFUL TOOL.

   Yes, I believe caps lock was necessary. It's like reading a book about getting healthy and losing weight while you're eating a bag of potato chips and drinking a soda. Simply *reading* about something won't make it happen.

   If you purchased this book, you should be open to new ideas and be ready to start putting new practices into place. Your LinkedIn results will improve if you are ready to learn and ready to take action.

   And, if you bought this book for your entire team, well– you've got to lead by example. They are going to look to you for affirmation and to demonstrate that this actually works.

4. **You also believe you can have fun while learning.** I mean, *obviously*. Otherwise, what the heck are you doing with a book

called, *Social Media Pie*? That's crazy talk, right? Or is it BRIL-LIANT? Probably a bit of both, but I'm glad you picked this up and I look forward to having a BLAST with you along the way.

My favorite pie is Banana Cream Pie – it is a family
favorite, although my son loves sweet potato.
- Sarah Tyler
www.linkedin.com/in/sarah-tyler-35180b55

Chapter 2:

Who This Book Is For & How This Book Can Help You

"We must have a pie.
Stress cannot exist in the presence of a pie."
~ David Mamet,
Boston Marriage

Everyone in this world has talent and expertise. If you have the opportunity and drive to figure out what your passion is and you're able to turn it into a career, you won't ever feel like you're working. Well, it might still feel like work sometimes but I know that since I've become an independent consultant, Mondays feel way less "Monday-like."

I love LinkedIn. And I'm *very* passionate about the power and potential of LinkedIn. This book was written by me for you. I know there are some authors who have ghostwriters working for them. Not me! With me, you get my thoughts directly from the source: *me.*

Ever since joining LinkedIn, I've made discoveries along the way that have helped my career, my clients, my consulting business, and my LinkedIn community.

For years, I've been talking about my goal of writing a LinkedIn book and I'm thrilled this day – and this book! – is finally here.

If you're reading this, you want to improve your LinkedIn efforts and results. While this book can have many applications for many audiences, I ultimately designed and wrote it so you could better understand the magic of this awesome network and figure out how to make that magic work for you.

My goal for you is that, throughout your reading and hopefully long after, you will be INSPIRED.

This isn't intended to be leisurely reading, though you may find my stories and my fascination with pie to be entertaining. Truth be told, I even find it amusing.

I wrote these words for you so you can realize the value of the investment in not only purchasing this book but the time you're spending on LinkedIn.

There are many other LinkedIn books out there, and I've read (or listened to) many of them.

Part of what held me back from getting started was trying to figure out what my unique angle would be for this book's focus. I wanted to make sure I had something different and interesting to offer to my readers.

Then it hit me: what makes me different is MY unique point of view. That, and my love of pie. Today, I'm sharing social media pie with you.

Do you work in business development?

That's great! This book is PERFECT for you! I'm going to offer you insights and strategies to help you take your LinkedIn activity from the slow lane to the super highway. You may have picked this book up because you're already pretty savvy on LinkedIn. You may have even thought about putting it back down because you think you know everything there is to know about LinkedIn.

But then a nagging feeling set in. Maybe this was driven in part because you're on LinkedIn nearly every day, sometimes several times a day, but your posts aren't getting any engagement. Or maybe they are getting a few likes here and there, but that's it.

Forget about leads: you're simply not finding them on LinkedIn, and you don't know why.

Maybe your invitation approach isn't working. I'm sure there are a few of you reading this right now who are using LinkedIn invitation automation services.

> SPOILER ALERT: I don't recommend them. LinkedIn will work best if you're genuine and authentic. I prefer a personalized or at least semi-personalized approach that involves you reading each profile before you connect, even if it's just for 10-15 seconds. And please don't make the invitation *about you* or a sales pitch for your business. More on this later...

Again, if your LinkedIn efforts are working so well, why are you reading this? My guess is because you know you could be doing *better*. My goal is that every sales leader, sales team member, or sales trainee reading this book will gain new insights to supercharge your lead generation efforts. And, even if your boss gave you this book and told you to read it, you gave it a chance and were pleasantly surprised by the end. If I'm right, send me a message on LinkedIn right now: www.linkedin.com/in/brendameller

Are you a company leader?

That's great! Perhaps you saw me speak at an event or you're following me on LinkedIn. You see the power of the personal brand I'm developing on LinkedIn, and you were intrigued. You are active on LinkedIn, but you can't figure out why your team isn't using LinkedIn to its full potential.

You know if they *did* then they could be activated as brand ambassadors to help your sales team do more. You realize there's some hesitation they have, but you're not quite sure what it is or how to get past it.

My goal for you is that, by the end of this book, you'll be convinced enough about the effectiveness of my strategies that you share this book with your second-in-command, or perhaps even your entire leadership team.

You know that there are a few of them who won't read it, but others will, and perhaps that will create momentum for the others to follow along.

The book itself is going to be such an awesome resource for you, and I've written it with *you* in mind.

Are you in a career transition or in-between successes?

First of all, I have got to tell you something. If you're in-between successes and not working right now, I want you to know that I BELIEVE IN YOU. This is temporary. You will find another job. And, even if you're not working, you'll always have that experience wherever you go.

If you're in a career transition that isn't by choice, there are understandably many emotions involved. You may swing from anger to relief to panic to happiness all in the same day. I know because I've been there myself.

My advice for you is to allow yourself to feel every emotion, especially at the beginning of your journey. Bottling things up inside isn't a good idea. It will all come out eventually; holding back your emotions could be hindering your career prospects.

The last career transition I had was in the summer of 2017; I recall crying fat, big tears the first few days. My husband would find me crying on our patio swing and he'd try to console me. And I told him what I'll tell you: I needed to FEEL those emotions to let go of them. I'm glad I did, because that's part of what propelled my consulting career forward and led in part to writing this book.

If you truly loved your job and your company, there is an emotional process you need to go through when you leave. It's similar to a mourning process. You have lost something; what you're feeling is normal.

At some point though, you need to wipe away the tears, take a deep breath, and press forward.

I strongly believe that energy moves in one direction. You can either focus that energy on the past and negative feelings of anger, betrayal, resentment, fear, or sadness, or you can focus your energy forward on YOU and YOUR FUTURE.

The more time you spend on the past, the less time you spend on YOU and the current version of yourself. And remember, I BELIEVE IN YOU.

You carry your experiences with you wherever you go. Sure, you may have to turn in your security badge, your laptop (it was really *their* laptop), your phone (it was really *their* phone), and leave with a box or two of your personal belongings... but your *experience* isn't something you have to leave there too.

You are not your job title. You are the culmination of your experiences. You are your passion. You are your insights and your expertise. You carry with you your institutional knowledge and industry expertise. I'm going to guide you on how to drive all of that awesomeness into your LinkedIn profile.

Perhaps you'll be one of those who send me "the note" after you land a new position, with this book having helped you along the way.

What's "the note", you ask? Well, it was inspired by a person I met years ago after delivering a LinkedIn training workshop to individuals in career transition. He sent me an email titled "The Note" and shared news that he had found a job.

If you can visualize yourself sending *the note*, my belief is that your mind will figure out a way for you to make it happen.

If you are in career transition and in-between successes, it's important that YOU believe in yourself, too, and keep that belief in mind as you're reading through this book. These strategies will work for you while you're in job search mode and beyond.

Are you considering a future career transition and looking to subtly ramp up your LinkedIn for a job search?

That's great! You don't have to admit who you are. In fact, it's better if we both approach this from the perspective that you bought this book to enhance your professional brand (WINK WINK).

I've used LinkedIn while working for employers, positioning myself for my next move. I call this, 'Using LinkedIn in Stealth Mode' (more on this later).

My advice for you is this: Instead of scaling back your support for your current employer, amp it up. Demonstrate that you are one of the company's biggest cheerleaders and advocates. Do this for the sake of the business, not the boss who frustrates you.

By doing so, your current employer will have NO IDEA you're looking to make a move. On the contrary, they will be so pleased that you are helping them.

Oh, and your competitors? They'll notice you too. After all, if you're going to add a new member to your team, wouldn't you want to hire someone who is a great brand ambassador? If they're doing such a great job promoting their CURRENT organization, chances are they will do so for your company, too!

Have you started (or are you currently running) your own business?

That's great! After I made the decision to choose an entrepreneurial path rather than search for another corporate job, I never looked back. I also found an amazing community of fellow entrepreneurs who openly share insights and resources with each other through my LinkedIn network and referrals.

I met people like Tammy Pereira (www.linkedin.com/in/tammypereira), who taught me the importance of following up on proposals. "That's YOUR Money! Go after it!," she said during a coffee meeting one cold January morning. She also introduced me to the book, Profit First by Mike Michalowicz (www.linkedin.com/in/mikemichalowicz). This book taught me a money management approach for my business that has been one key of my success.

As an entrepreneur, I know you're passionate about what you do. You're resourceful. You're willing to take chances. You're wearing many hats. And you aren't afraid to say when you need help. This book is for you.

I'll bring you my insights as a marketer AND as an entrepreneur! And I'll teach you strategic ways to grow your network to help you grow your business. And how to surround yourself with your biggest cheerleaders and fellow entrepreneurs, like Crystal Anderson (www.linkedin.com/in/crystalandersoncmp).

> Side note: I tell people that I'm "enthusiastically unemployable" – which means I love being an entrepreneur SO MUCH that there's no salary offer that could convince me to return to being an employee. (If you also identify as "enthusiastically unemployable," you're welcome to join my LinkedIn group: *www.linkedin.com/groups/8805332.*)

Have you been following me on LinkedIn? Or maybe you're one of my connections or supporters...

That's great and you are AWESOME! One of the things I love most about LinkedIn is the community it's created for me. I am always so happy to hear when the insights I share can help others.

Some people don't have the budget or desire to book me for individual coaching or to attend one of my conferences or events. I get it and I'm totally cool with it. That's one reason I wrote this book: for those of you on a budget and who are open to a guided DIY approach for LinkedIn.

But guess what? Even if there's not a specific business or career reason you're reading this book, this book will help you. You may keep it afterwards for reference, or you may pass it along to someone else in your network to pay it forward and help them. You'll be sharing it with others and building social media karma on LinkedIn.

And that is what social media pie is all about!

My favorite pie is Apple Pie!
- Jordan Rae
www.linkedin.com/in/jordanrrrae

Chapter 3:

Why I Love Pie

"Well we're movin on up,
To the east side.
To a deluxe apartment in the sky.
Movin on up
To the east side.
We finally got a piece of the pie."
~ Ja'Net DuBois,
theme song to "The Jeffersons"

My name is Brenda Meller and I love pie. Every now and again, people ask if I *truly* love pie, and if so, why?

First of all, *yes I do*.

When I was younger, my mom would enter baking contests at the Michigan State Fair every summer. She loved to bake. I grew up thinking everyone's mom loved to bake and that everyone's family participated in summer baking contests.

One summer, there was a mother-daughter pie baking competition. This was a live contest, one in which we would have to be at the State Fair on a particular day and time to present the pie together.

I was maybe 12 or 13 at the time. I remember my mom and I wore coordinated outfits on that particular day. I wore black pants and a white blazer and she wore white pants and a black blazer. I remember taking a photo outside of our house, the two of us standing in the hot summer sun proudly holding the apple pie we'd baked together.

When we arrived at the State Fair, we had competition. The judges tasted each pie and then scored them.

We didn't win that day. The winning pie was a unique combination that stood out from the others.

Ours was a classic apple pie with a homemade crust. It was my mom's homemade recipe, but there wasn't any "zinger" to it.

That was OK for both of us. While we had signed up to try to win, we both just really loved cooking and it was something fun for us to do together.

That's what pie is for me: something you enjoy with others.

My mom passed away in 1998 from cervical cancer (ladies: get your annual pap exams). She had a 2-3 year battle from the disease, and passed away when she was 46. I was just 24 at the time.

I didn't know it then, but the pie-baking contest we participated in would go on to become one of my most vivid and loving memories of my mom and me.

Years passed before I started to realize my true love of pie– I think it has something to do with that competition!

There are warm memories of my family and fun, happy times. I wish I could find that picture of the two of us with the pie in front of our house. I'll keep digging around and maybe it will present itself!

So, when did I first start talking about my love of pie and weaving it into my LinkedIn presentations? Probably just a few years ago.

I recall one presentation I gave at the Sterling Heights Regional Chamber (SHRCCI) at Dave & Busters that really propelled things forward.

Every slide featured an ingredient (like bananas), and then the next slide showed a pie made with that ingredient (banana cream pie).

I invited attendees to post on social media using the hashtag, #social-mediapie, partially just to have fun and tie in with the presentation, and partially because it wasn't a heavily used hashtag and it would be easy for me to come back and find those mentions later.

A handful of people DID use the hashtag that night. And then something magical started to happen... they *kept* using it!

Pam Abdelnour of Tedesco Services attended (*www.linkedin.com/in/pame laabdelnour*) and blogged about the event, using the hashtag in her piece. You can read it here: tedescoservices.com/social-media -marketing-pie-combine

A month or so later, people who were there that night were STILL tagging me on LinkedIn with the #socialmediapie hashtag.

At this point, I realized something special was happening.

I then did what any smart marketer would do: I reserved "social media pie" across all four major social media platforms (Facebook, Instagram, LinkedIn, and Twitter) and reserved the website socialmediapie.com, redirecting it to my personal website, mellermarketing.com.

I didn't know why at the time. I just knew I should do it.

A few months after the SHRCCI event, I was in a conversation with Terry Bean (www.linkedin.com/in/terrybean) about his Motor City Connect group. We met at Grand Traverse Pie in Troy, one of my favorite places for pie in Metro Detroit.

At the end of lunch, as we were walking back to our cars, I asked Terry about speakers for his upcoming events. I can't recall if I offered to be a speaker or if he had asked me.

Either way, I didn't want to commit to anything unless it was going to be entertaining and informative; I also didn't want to step on his turf. Terry is a fellow LinkedIn expert, trainer, and coach, among other things.

I mentioned my love of pie and that it was something I was kicking around in my head as a talk. He thought it sounded fun. Within the next day or so, I drafted an outline of my talk and shared it with him, and Terry signed me up to be the next month's speaker.

This is the outline I used for my talk:

1. Do you remember the baking contest at the Michigan State Fair?
2. I don't really like _____. For me, it's cake or cupcakes.
3. Pie is for sharing. Not like bacon or a cupcake.
4. Pie is like marketing because your central idea is your filling.
5. Pie is like marketing because the crust (what we see) can make or break a good pie.
6. Have you ever been to a pie-up?
7. One day, #socialmediapie was born.
8. People love free stuff. Especially pie.
9. What makes YOU happy to talk about, unrelated to work or your business?
10. Remember me on #PieDayFriday, Thanksgiving, and the next time you see pie at any social gathering.

Thanks to Roy Sexton (www.linkedin.com/in/royesexton) who attended that day and captured photos, as can be seen at: www.instagram.com/p/BnB4fFxAYvw/

My talk inspired the theme and title of this book and I'm happy to share this story with you.

Pie is my *thing*– which I'm sure you've gathered by now! Pie has nothing to do with LinkedIn, at least not in a direct way. My clients and customers know I love pie. They know I light up when I bring pie to an event to give away. And I see that THEY light up when they see the pie I've brought.

My love of pie is also mentioned in my "about" statement on LinkedIn. I suggest that when people connect with me, they mention what their favorite pie is. You'll see some of these mentions throughout this book at the end of each chapter.

What I've realized is that my love of pie has helped me to differentiate myself from my competition– even on LinkedIn!

Pie makes me happy but, while I've made a conscious effort to tie it into my business, it's not really related to what I do.

My advice to you? Find something you *love*. Now think about how you could weave it into your business. Make that YOUR social media pie.

It's safe to say my online brand now includes pie. Chances are, after reading this book, you'll remember me *and* my love of pie, too. That's the power of social media and developing a personal brand with some fun and personality.

Per your about section, my favorite pie is pecan.
~ Karl Pyka
www.linkedin.com/in/karl-pyka

Chapter 4:

Pie and LinkedIn

*"Cut my pie into four pieces,
I don't think I could eat eight."*
~ *Yogi Berra*

So, how does one weave the theme of "pie" into an online professional site like LinkedIn? In my case, it happened without my even knowing it. Pie is something I love, and one day it took on a life of its own in my LinkedIn journey.

There are LITERAL mentions of pie in this book and on my LinkedIn profile, and there's the ESSENCE of social media pie, and I'll serve each one in a tidy slice for you.

LITERAL PIE on LinkedIn

As mentioned previously, when I started weaving my love of pie into presentations and I started using the hashtag #socialmediapie, it started to develop a life of its own.

People started using the hashtag when they were tagging me in posts on items that they thought might interest me. Sometimes, the items were just about LinkedIn and had nothing to do with me personally.

Other times, the posts were related to pie humor, pie facts, and even pie holidays (there are a whole BUNCH of them listed by the National Day Calendar and, yes, I try to celebrate them all!).

Sometimes, I'll share these pie holiday celebrations on LinkedIn.

"But Brenda," you say, "LinkedIn is a professional network and I've heard that we should not post the same things on LinkedIn that you post on Facebook."

You are absolutely correct. When you are posting on LinkedIn, you have to consider that the average user is in business mode. It's as if they are picking up a newspaper like *The Wall Street Journal* or *The New York Times*. They are seeking *business* information.

However, unlike with these publications, they are often reading about people they know, people like me and you, on LinkedIn.

What makes LinkedIn so powerful in part is that we can build professional relationships online, and a part of doing that is establishing *trust*.

People want to do business with REAL people. And that means it's OK if you occasionally pull back the professional front and reveal bits of your personality.

I'm not heavily promoting my love of pie on LinkedIn, but there are little glimpses on my LinkedIn profile. For example, if you read my "about" statement, you'll see at the end that I say: "HOW TO CONNECT WITH ME: Tell me your favorite pie."

Do people actually follow this tip? Sometimes they do!

I recently searched for "my favorite pie is" in my LinkedIn box to find these messages, and then I messaged each person to let them know they would be getting a shout-out in my book when it was published. One person,

Susanna Brennan (www.linkedin.com/in/susannabrennan1), suggested I hold my book launch party on March 14, 2020 (pie day). While that party didn't happen due to COVID-19, it was a brilliant idea on her part.

A little further up in my LinkedIn profile, I also sprinkle in some philosophies that include mentions of pie. These are a blend of well-known quotes and quotes I've modified a bit to suit my personality. For example, "When life hands you lemons, make a lemon pie."

That's really about it. My love of pie isn't all-consuming in my LinkedIn activity nor in my LinkedIn profile. It's just a sprinkling to add some flavor of my personality to my page.

My use of "pie" on my LinkedIn profile is similar to the amount of salt you would use in a pie recipe. It's only there to enhance the flavor of the pie. Add too much salt and you've ruined the pie. Not enough or skip the salt altogether and your pie might taste like it's missing something!

Social Media Pie: **The essence of pie in sweet, single-serve slices.**

Okay, so now that you know I'm not suggesting you share pie recipes as posts or articles on LinkedIn, let's talk about the ESSENCE of what I mean by "social media pie."

A pie is for sharing. It is meant to be enjoyed by a group. I've seen a pie sliced into eight perfect slices using special bakery tools. I used to work at Sign of the Beefcarver, and I remember the servers slicing pies up so perfectly.

Of course, you might share a pie with more than eight people. Think about Thanksgiving dessert time. Everybody is full, but everybody is also looking forward to dessert.

I can still hear my grandma Sophie saying, "Just a tiny slice. A little bit of each." This was how much pie she wanted after we played Monopoly or Scrabble to let our Thanksgiving dinner settle.

I'm not even going to suggest you try to eat a whole pie in one sitting because that's just crazy talk... *unless* you're in a pie eating contest.

Pie filling is rich. Pie crust is high in calories. Sure, it's delicious, but it's even more enjoyable when you are sharing it with and enjoying it with others.

> FUN FACT: When I was in college, I was a waitress at a Big Boy Restaurant. I noticed that when customers ordered a slice of pie and I would serve it to them, they would always turn the pie so the point was facing them and they'd eat from the point.
>
> The pie is pointing at you! This is the essence of social media pie on LinkedIn. You, dear reader, will be pointing your posts toward other people (at least MOST of the time). This is what will make your LinkedIn posts a success.

Selling to a person is NOT the same as directing a post toward a person. Nobody wants to be sold to. Everybody likes shopping, and we enjoy buying if we see something of value that we need or want. But nobody likes a bunch of sales pitches clogging up their LinkedIn homepage feed.

One thing I'd suggest you start to do is pay attention to your homepage feed. You may notice that there are some posts which are performing really well. I like to call this the "trade show" effect.

Imagine you're at a trade show. All those desperate salespeople are watching as you walk briskly by their tables. You're trying not to make eye contact, because you know they are desperate to make a sale.

But then, you see a table and something interesting is happening. People are gathering around. They are laughing, smiling, talking with one another. There may even be a small crowd forming. Your curiosity is piqued. You are *interested*. What IS going on at that table? Is that a prize wheel?

You step in for a closer look…

The same thing happens on the LinkedIn homepage feed. A post starts to perform well by generating a few likes (reactions) and a few comments. And the more engagement it generates, the more people who see the post. The more people who see the post, the more potential reach it creates. And then more likes, more comments.

Before you know it, that post is reaching hundreds and then thousands and then tens of thousands of people.

Want to know one of my secrets? Sure you do, or you wouldn't have bought this book, right?

When I see a post that's performing well, and:

1. It aligns with my values,
2. I believe in the person who posted it, and
3. I find the message interesting,

I will take a moment to like it and add a comment of five or more words. This is a magical number on LinkedIn. If you comment, "great post!" or "congratulations!" on a post, it doesn't really help to keep that post in the homepage feed very long.

When you comment with, "This reminds me of a manager I used to work with who always inspired me to be my best. He loved the New York Yankees and used a lot of baseball analogies," or some other variation of five or more words, it helps that post to stay in the homepage feed longer.

A longer comment is the equivalent of another pair of people hanging around that trade show table, attracting more people to the table.

Want to take it a step further? End your comment with a question that prompts a response. Continuing from my example above, the question might be, "Do you live in New York or do you love the Yankees, too?"

If you're posting engaging, believable, genuine, and interesting content, then you are creating social media pie and everyone is going to want a slice.

My favorite pie is warm apple crumble!!
And it's totally that time of year!!
~ Miranda VonFricken
www.linkedin.com/in/mirandavonfricken

Chapter 5:

My LinkedIn Journey

"Pies mean Thanksgiving and Christmas and picnics."
~ Janet Clarkson, Pie: A Global History

Several years ago, I was ready to make a career move. There was no room for career growth at my employer, and I wanted to move up. I had hit the proverbial glass ceiling and I knew I had gone as far as I could go within the company.

I tried changing things for a while. After writing what I referred to as my "Jerry Maguire letter" to the president of the company about the importance of employee engagement on the bottom line, I was given approval to form a new cross-functional employee group called the Employee Engagement Board (EEB).

But I was STILL hitting brick wall after brick wall in my desire to be promoted into a position of leadership.

The year was 2008. It was the height of a recession in Michigan, and the absolute worst time for someone who was fully employed to decide to make a job change.

Both Michigan and Metro Detroit were flooded with thousands of displaced workers due to the economic downturn.

My competition included people who could dedicate ALL of their waking hours to searching for a new job. I had a full-time job, a long commute, and a family, leaving me with little time to look.

Plus, I dreaded the "black hole" that comes with using platforms like Monster and HotJobs to find a new career. Anyone who has ever searched for a new job knows what I mean. The "black hole" is the soul-sucking, endless void that you experience when you apply to job after job with NO responses, save for an occasional auto-reply.

I knew I would have to approach my search differently.

I was already on LinkedIn, thanks to the advice of a coworker and mentor, Erika Crocker (www.linkedin.com/in/erika-crocker-1372a54).

However, I saw that LinkedIn offered a new path for my search. I decided to step up my efforts on LinkedIn. I disconnected from my boss and the president of the company, to reduce the risk of them knowing of my impending move. Truth be told, they weren't very active on LinkedIn anyway, and I doubt they noticed.

I vowed to myself at the time to avoid the job boards, which were flooded by job seekers for a handful of job openings. Based on past job searches, I found it too difficult and depressing. I wanted action. And I HATED the soul-crushing, energy-sucking job search loop.

I looked at LinkedIn daily, and one day, I found it: a job posting for a 'Marketing Manager' at a local college.

It was a perfect match for me. It required a passion for professional development and experience in marketing. I was so excited!

I applied through HR and then I also decided to upgrade my LinkedIn membership to make a direct connection to the hiring manager who posted the position. (I would later tell people this was the best $30 I've ever spent!)

The hiring manager told me mine was the first resume he received on LinkedIn, out of the hundreds of resumes the posting had generated.

This didn't even include the hundreds of resumes from the Monster posting, or those sent directly to the HR department.

Within a day or so, he emailed me to set up an interview and we met within a week. The rest, as they say, is history.

If it wasn't for LinkedIn, I wouldn't be where I am today.

If it wasn't for the approach I used to find that job on LinkedIn, you wouldn't be reading this book!

It's *that* powerful. And I will forever be repaying this back to help others.

Fast forward to today. I've now been on LinkedIn for nearly 15 years, and I've always been active on the network. Part of the reason I've had such great success sharing my insights with others is that I've spent a lot of time observing, testing new techniques, and learning from others (both their successes and mistakes).

As a marketer, I've always kept a focus on my business goals and my intended target audience, and have considered how my LinkedIn activities are supporting both areas.

I've used LinkedIn as a job seeker, a marketer, a company ambassador, a member of an organization's leadership team, a hiring manager, a coach/mentor, a working professional, a board member, a consultant, a speaker, and now as an author.

I've mainly used the free version of LinkedIn, but for the past few years I've upgraded to LinkedIn Premium to access additional features that help me in my business.

I recently upgraded to LinkedIn Sales Navigator to check out the additional features for my business, as well as to help support my clients who purchased this subscription level.

However, whenever I'm working with a new client, I always bring up the conversation about investing in LinkedIn Premium or LinkedIn Sales Navigator. I want to be sure that people understand how to maximize the *free* version before upgrading.

I make no money by recommending that my clients upgrade to LinkedIn Premium or Sales Navigator.

It's common that when I ask people who have LinkedIn Premium *why* they have it and *how* they are using it, they don't know.

Sometimes their employer is paying for it, so they really don't care much about the money. Others remember LinkedIn offering them a free 1-month trial, and, now, they barely notice the $59.99 monthly bill. They are afraid that if they cancel it, they'll lose access to features they are using, but they aren't really sure what those features are. It's classic FOMO (the Fear Of Missing Out).

I'd rather see you focus your efforts on optimizing your profile, growing your network with dialog, and engaging with people while building your brand on your homepage feed first– THEN upgrade to Premium if and when you hit a wall to access features that you need.

> *This book can help, and I only charge you one fee, one time. But feel free to send me a check every month, or buy more copies of this book, if you feel so inclined! :)*

The first feature people usually want to access is: "Who Viewed Your Profile." Yes, this can be a powerful feature, but if you're not sending personalized invitations, your chances of people accepting your invitations are pretty low. And if your profile isn't optimized, the wrong people could be looking at your profile. Not *bad* people. But those who are not your ideal target audience– so why bother inviting them to connect?

The other feature I use in Premium is 'unlimited searches.' Now keep in mind that a core of my business is LinkedIn coaching and training, so I'm looking up hundreds of profiles each month. The average person may not be searching for as many people on LinkedIn.

There are a few other cool features on LinkedIn Premium that are valuable to me. One is the ability to do a Live Chat with someone from 'LinkedIn Help.' This has enabled me to find fast solutions for myself and for my clients when I get stumped.

The free InMail Messages that come with LinkedIn Premium are really not that useful to me. As of right now, I have 43 unused InMail credits. I currently get 15 more InMail credits per month.[1]

I've also accessed the free on-demand videos through LinkedIn Learning, which are helpful but I'm not sure I would miss them.

I started with just one LinkedIn connection and then two, and then one day I had 50, and a while after that, I had 500+ showing on my profile.

I'm focusing on *growing* my network every day, and you should, too.

LinkedIn has been a platform that has enabled me to make a career change. It has led me to meet awesome mentors, to find perfect job

---

1   FYI I found this information here: www.linkedin.com/premium/my-premium which appears to be a link that works if you have LinkedIn premium. It shows you all your LinkedIn premium features.

candidates, to locate much needed vendors, to position me to be found by clients, and to build my continually evolving personal brand.

I had started doing some side work based on requests that were coming my way and I decided to set up an LLC and a website for Meller Marketing, as part of a graduate class project.

Right around this time, I had a breakfast meeting at Recipes Restaurant with Terry Barclay (www.linkedin.com/in/terrybarclay), who told me I could definitely build my own business as a LinkedIn coach and consultant. I told her she was crazy. Well, she was right.

When I left my last corporate position, I had established my personal brand so well that my business started to take off almost immediately and with little effort on my own in the beginning.

In fact, the leads and inquiries were coming in before I even knew I would become a full-time independent marketing consultant.

My career path chose me, thanks to LinkedIn.

I wasn't someone who had dreamed and planned of leaving my corporate job to work on my own. I had admired those people for years, but I never thought I could be one of them.

The universe sometimes has a funny way of nudging us forward, and when I found myself evaluating where to go next, I discovered that there was a demand for my expertise.

People reached out to me through LinkedIn, text, and email to meet for coffee and lunch.

One person after another said, "Hey Brenda. Since you have time, could you help me with my LinkedIn? Hey Brenda, since you have time, could you help me with my social media for my company? Hey Brenda, since you have time, could you help my company with marketing?"

I quickly realized that my expertise was seen as highly valuable and it was sought after, and I wasn't even trying to market myself for these services.

At the time, I had zero fear about where the future would lead. Why? Because I believed in myself. I knew my potential, my drive, and my desire to succeed. I knew I would never let myself down, and the only thing holding me back was my confidence in myself.

And when I leaned into my consulting business in the beginning of 2018, things quickly escalated and I discovered I had a solid foundation and platform for growth.

I was already starting to do a lot of public speaking in my professional career, thanks to my years of Toastmasters – a nonprofit educational organization that operates clubs worldwide for the purpose of promoting communication, public speaking and leadership – along with my desire to work through my introverted personality and develop confidence speaking in front of groups.

In the past year, I have spoken at two national conferences and over 100 other events. I'm expanding my focus on public speaking in the coming years, and LinkedIn will be a platform for that growth.

I've also been coaching hundreds of individuals, dozens of teams, and thousands of conference attendees on how to unlock the power of LinkedIn.

I've had "write a LinkedIn book" as a personal goal on my LinkedIn profile for several years, and LinkedIn led me to a connection, Michael Dwyer, who heard me speak at a 'Lunch and Learn' event for Oakland Community College.

Michael reached out and asked me to speak at the 2019 Rochester Writer's Conference, where I met Don Staley, the author of "*How to Write a Book in 30 Days*," which has led me to you… or is it that it led you to me?

My LinkedIn journey, while well-established, feels in some ways like it has just begun.

My guess is that you're reading this book because you are ready for LinkedIn to support you in the next phase of your journey.

You may be using LinkedIn to find a new job and you're in a career transition / in-between success.

You may be using LinkedIn to establish or expand your personal brand, as you think about planting the seeds for your future career.

You may be using LinkedIn as an entrepreneur or salesperson, to find leads.

You may be a social media manager or even one of my fellow 'LinkedIn Rockstars,' looking to learn from a peer. That's perfectly OK with me. In fact, it's more than OK. I'm flattered!

You may be one of my many supporters who has been propelling me forward every step of the way. And, if so, I thank you every day! We should celebrate with virtual coffee and pie!

You may be one of the many people I've mentioned in this book. How cool! I want YOUR autograph on that page of the book when we meet.

Before I began my journey of writing a book, I got my hands on as many LinkedIn books as I could. My goal was to figure out how to write a book that was uniquely me and one that could benefit YOU.

I am a big believer in the 'abundance mentality'. There is more than enough work to go around for all of us. My friend Terry Bean calls it "coopetition" while fellow LinkedIn coach Elisa Bennett calls it a "restaurant row" strategy. By supporting each other and surrounding ourselves with our competitors, we can all achieve *more*.

Whatever led you to this book, I hope to be a critical part of your success on your LinkedIn journey.

I'm a big fan of affirmations, so I invite you to take a moment now to write an affirmation about how LinkedIn will help you. Write it in the form of a positive statement and as if it's something you've *already* achieved.

For example, MY affirmation might be:

"I am enjoying reading my published, *New York Times* and Amazon bestselling Social Media Pie book, and the feedback from my readers who say this book has helped them rock on LinkedIn."

OR

"I am enjoying working just four hours a day because my bestselling book is bringing in passive income from worldwide sales, supplemented by my speaking business."

OR

"I am enjoying the lifestyle I have created from my books, my public speaking business, and my LinkedIn coaching practice and I love being *Enthusiastically Unemployable*. I have inspired others with the "Brenda Effect" to help them live out their dreams."

If you want something in life, you have to tell the universe what you want. Now, let's take YOU on the next step of YOUR LinkedIn journey, and enjoy some "social media pie" along the way.

My favorite pie is Lemon Pie.
~ Jean-Francois GEORGES
www.linkedin.com/in/jean-francois-georges-optimiste

Chapter 6:

How to WIN on LinkedIn

"You may receive a pie, eat it and forget. You may receive champagne, drink it and forget. But when you receive a book, you can open it again and again."
~ Israelmore Ayivor, 101 Keys To Everyday Passion

My guess is there is a handful of you who flipped right to this section looking for my insider tips to help you make big wins NOW on LinkedIn, *right*?

If so, sorry to disappoint you. There are no shortcuts.

Your LinkedIn success will be more akin to making a pumpkin pie from scratch rather than going to a McDonald's drive-thru to order a *McPumpkin Pie*.

Yes, you can WIN on LinkedIn, but it will take time, effort, and desire. LinkedIn is not a "set it and forget it" network where you can simply optimize your personal LinkedIn profile, optimize your LinkedIn company page, and then wait for the leads to pour in.

You will see results if you focus on LinkedIn in three critical areas. I like to keep things simple. Perhaps this P-I-E acronym will help you:

P = Profile Optimization. Optimizing your profile is something I'll go into greater detail in later chapters. Basically, it involves writing your profile for your IDEAL target audience and using all the content areas and considering the character limits and their impacts on LinkedIn search results.

I recommend you review and optimize your profile at least once a year. You change. Your job changes. Some of your information or content may even change and evolve as *you* change and evolve.

LinkedIn keeps changing, too. I noticed a steady increase of my "Who Viewed Your Profile" data up until the end of August 2019. Then it dropped, and then it dropped again. Then it returned. No, LinkedIn didn't tell us what changed. However, a bunch of us independent LinkedIn strategists compared notes. We heard the platform had deleted a bunch of spammy accounts. We also heard that the algorithm changed once again.

The good thing is that you have someone like me in your corner, and I'm always going to tell you what I know about profile optimization and when I'm making an educated guess based on my experience or intuition.

I = Invitation Strategy. I highly recommend you include a personal note in *every* LinkedIn invitation you send and make it all about the other person. Don't sell in your invitation and don't just click the "connect" button without including a note. More on this in Chapter 25. If you are including a personal note, you're doing two things:

1. Increasing the likelihood that the recipient will ACCEPT your invitation.

2. Establishing TRUST, an important basis for creating dialog, which may result in more dialog and lead you toward your business goals.

> **Yes, you have to personalize EVERY invitation EVERY time. It's just good manners.**

E = Engagement. I don't put a lot of guarantees in my book because I strongly believe that results vary and I don't want anyone thinking they are going to get their money back if my "guarantees" don't work.

But here's one guarantee I am comfortable making: I guarantee that if you only sell in your posts, if you ignore your homepage feed and rarely like or comment on other peoples' posts, if you only *request* recommendations and never *give* them, and if you are using LinkedIn selfishly, then I guarantee LinkedIn will NOT work for you.

All the expertise found in this book, on my social media accounts, and in my daily posts are based on my experience, analysis, and results.

Sometimes clients come to me because they are on LinkedIn all the time and they're still not getting any results.

Does that sound like you? Are you on LinkedIn all the time and not getting results? I can tell within about 60 seconds of reviewing your profile why that might be.

You won't WIN on LinkedIn if your profile has errors, is incomplete, or isn't optimized for your ideal target audience.

You won't WIN on LinkedIn if you send blind invites – *or even worse* – an invitation with a sales message included in the invitation message. Sure, you may pick up a client here and there but, overall, it's a numbers game and the odds will be stacked against you.

People don't like to be sold to. Some will not only ignore the invite, but they may click the "I don't know this person" button which is a one-way ticket to what I call 'LinkedIn Jail.'

You won't WIN on LinkedIn if you ignore your connections or people who engage with your posts or your company page posts. You won't. Nope.

Winning on LinkedIn is like making a homemade pumpkin pie. First, you have to bake a pumpkin and make a homemade crust. Then, let the baked pumpkin cool and add in the other ingredients for the filling. Then, bake the pie filling in the pre-baked crust. Wrap the crust with some foil (or it will burn), and watch it closely as it nears the done stage.

Let it cool and then savor that lovely slice of pie, bite by bite. Anyone else hungry?

You'll win when you follow the recipe closely, when you use quality ingredients, and when you watch the results every step of the way.

Ready to win? I'm ready to guide you.

My favorite pie is apple pie (or, appeltaart in Dutch).
~ Anoek Schippers
www.linkedin.com/in/anoekschippers

Section 2:

Settings & Privacy

Chapter 7:

Overview of Settings & Privacy Section

"Harry: Pepper.
Sally: Pepper.
Harry: Waiter, there is too much pepper on my paprikash.
Sally: Waiter, there is too much pepper on my paprikash.
Harry: But I would be proud to partake of your pecan pie."
~ Movie Scene from "When Harry Met Sally"

> NOTE: The chapters within this section are pretty dry, but they are necessary if you *really* want to optimize your time and effort on LinkedIn. Feel free to skim them for now, and spend some time on LinkedIn as you're reviewing these chapters later, OK?

Yes, it's a lot to cover, but something you only need to do once a year or so to make sure you are aware of your settings and how they can help or hinder you from achieving your goals on LinkedIn.

Oh, and you need to know your LinkedIn password for many of these settings. This is LinkedIn's way of making sure it's really YOU who wants to change these settings. If you don't know your password, it's probably time to change it. Just make sure you don't save your passwords in a folder on your desktop called PASSWORDS or write your passwords on a sticky note and put it under your computer keyboard. Don't make it easy for people to hack into your accounts.

The very first thing I do when working with a client to optimize his or her LinkedIn profile (after talking about their goals, challenges, and questions about LinkedIn) is to start by looking at the settings and privacy section. This is something you should review at least once a year.

LinkedIn is notorious for adjusting settings without telling users they've changed a default. Usually, the change works in our favor, but I've seen hiccups occur and new settings that may limit your profile visibility.

I recommend you access this area from the desktop version of LinkedIn. The mobile version (viewable on tablets and in the LinkedIn app) has some, but not ALL of the features as seen in the full desktop version.

Once you are logged into your account, click on the "ME" icon in the upper right corner of your top menu bar, then click the down arrow to make the menu appear.

Under "ACCOUNT," click on "Settings & Privacy."

There are multiple menus in the left navigation. I'll focus on the areas I've found to be the most relevant.

This is one of the areas of your profile where I'll add a disclaimer. These are my recommendations based on *my* view of LinkedIn at the time this book was sent to the publisher. At the time of writing this, LinkedIn was rolling out an updated navigation including some modifications to the navigation within Settings & Privacy. Everything is still there, but items are in a new location. I'm showing you recommendations based on the newest navigation.

You may have personal reasons to have different settings. My goal is to explain my recommendations and rationale, to help educate you about the features, and to provide you an explanation for my suggestions. Then, it's up to you to decide for yourself what to do.

I'm not the boss of you. I'm the boss of my kids (at least until they turn 18 and/or until they leave my house!). You're the boss of you. Or maybe your boss is the boss of you. But, when it comes to LinkedIn, you should be your own boss.

If I were you, I'd prop this book up and follow along on LinkedIn so you can make the edits as you go.

My favorite pie is banana cream.
~ Matt Marturano
www.linkedin.com/in/drmatthewmarturano

Chapter 8:

Account Preferences

Good apple pies are a considerable part
of our domestic happiness.
~ Jane Austen

Once you click on "account preferences," you'll see the left navigation shows you these current sections (subject to change by LinkedIn):

- ➤ **Profile information**
- ➤ **Site preferences**
- ➤ **Syncing options**
- ➤ **Subscriptions & payments**
- ➤ **Partners & services**
- ➤ **Account management**

Profile information

There is currently only one section within this area to review, "Name, location, and industry."

Name, location, and industry

When you click this option, it takes you to a section of your LinkedIn profile that is referred to as your 'top header card.' There are only two areas I recommend you adjust. We'll review the other areas (headline, etc.) later.

Locations within this area

I recommend you set this as the *greater metro area* of where you live rather than your hometown city or the city where your workplace is located. By expanding it to the greater metro area (you can do this by clicking the dropdown arrow to adjust – if you've entered your zip or postal code, it will automatically pull up the nearest large metro area), you will come up in more searches for people across that greater metro area.

If you keep it as your hometown, you may be missing on some opportunities from search, as you appear in search results closest to your hometown, and not from across town. This may be important if you're in a highly competitive industry where there are a lot of people in your metro area. Plus, I don't need all LinkedIn members to know my hometown. Fraser is awesome, but it means nothing to someone outside of Michigan. The Detroit Metropolitan Area means a lot more to my connections throughout the U.S. and overseas.

Industry

You can only choose one industry designation for your personal LinkedIn profile. It doesn't appear anywhere on your profile, but it does help you to come up in more searches related to that industry. So, if you worked as a marketer at a university, your organization's industry would be **Higher Education**, but your personal industry of expertise might be **Marketing & Advertising.** I typically tell my clients to choose the industry that they want to be found in search results.

If you are in a sales role, I would choose the industry of your employer's products and services, so that your profile appears when someone is searching for those keywords or that product category.

If you're struggling with which industry to choose, I recommend you choose the industry of your employer, and look on your LinkedIn company page – or your top competitors' LinkedIn company pages – where the industry is shown.

> BONUS TIP: Want to come up in different searches? Try changing out your industry every month or so and include industries of your target audience.

Site preferences

The only settings I recommend you adjust here is within "Viewers of this profile also viewed." However, feel free to review the other areas, if you wish!

Viewers of this profile also viewed

I recommend you set this to "No" so that you aren't showing other peoples' profiles next to yours when they are on your LinkedIn profile.

If you're looking for a LinkedIn coach and you've landed on my profile, I don't want to send you to my competition. They are all lovely people but if you're on *my* profile, I want to keep you there.

In this day and age of social media, we all have short attention spans, and if we've gone through all the trouble of building a profile that people visit, why would you allow any optional information on the same page which could divert their attention?

Subscriptions & payments

➤ **Premium subscription**
➤ **View purchase history**

Premium subscription

I don't work for LinkedIn; I work for myself and I work for *you*. My goal is to help YOU optimize your time and effort on LinkedIn, and also to make sure you're not missing any opportunities. I also don't like to see people waste money.

Sometimes when I meet with executives, we discover they have a LinkedIn Premium account. To be fair, most of the time they KNOW they have LinkedIn Premium, but they have no idea what it is or what it does for them.

> I think the name "Premium" makes some people feel like they are getting the BEST version of LinkedIn. It very well may be worth it, but try changing the names to see how it changes your perception:
>
> Instead of calling it Basic LinkedIn, call it "FREE LinkedIn."
>
> Instead of calling it LinkedIn Premium, call it "PAID LinkedIn."

OK, so now that you know that you – or maybe your boss or your company – are paying for it, what value are you GETTING out of your investment in LinkedIn Premium?

I get value out of LinkedIn Premium just about every day. But the average user on LinkedIn isn't even using the FREE version of LinkedIn to its fullest potential. I speak from experience.

Giving the average person LinkedIn Premium would be like giving my 15-year-old son a Tesla when he turns 16 and hasn't taken driver's training yet. Why give him something with power when he doesn't even know how to back out of the driveway yet? Not to mention, I don't even drive a Tesla!

I recommend you only upgrade to LinkedIn Premium when all four of the below items have been met, and in this order:

1. **You have a fully optimized LinkedIn profile.** If you don't know what this means, read all chapters in Section 3 of this book.

2. **You personalize every invitation you send** and take a few moments to review and/or screen in every invitation you receive (at more than face value).

3. **You are engaging with people on your homepage feed (likes, comments) and you are posting** on a regular basis (at least once a week but ideally once per business day) and you are monitoring your comments and replying back.

4. **You are hitting roadblocks in features you want access to,** which are only available to premium members (such as unlimited profile searches).

If you have LinkedIn Premium and you have no idea what any of these items mean, I recommend you cancel Premium. You can always upgrade again later. Stop throwing money into access you're not even using.

Then, visit mellermarketing.com/thanksbrenda to pay me, instead! :)

But in all seriousness, please know that:

> *Premium does not mean better. Premium means you pay LinkedIn for additional features.*

Now don't get me wrong, I understand that LinkedIn is a business and they need to have a business model in place where they are bringing in revenue. What I don't like to see is people wasting money. I'd rather see you using the *free* version until you're done with driver's training, you've completed your requisite number of hours driving with a parent, you have all A's in school, and you have enough money in the bank to pay for your car payment (unless your Dad gives you his Subaru Forester), your monthly insurance, your gas, and any other expenses like taking your girlfriend out for a date. Oh, and make sure you buy your mom a piece of pie every now and again and give her a kiss on the cheek, too.

(I just read this out to my son and he said, "All A's in school? That's a bit of a stretch." So, there's that.)

My point is that you should earn the right and privilege to get access to LinkedIn Premium, and not just throw money at the people at LinkedIn.

You can throw money at them later, when you are rocking your business because of all these great strategies I'm teaching you, and you can "make it rain" with those wads of cash you are bringing in.

What types of Premium services does LinkedIn offer?
At the time of publication of this book, here's what LinkedIn offers:

> ➤ LinkedIn Premium Career for $29.99/month (or $239.88/year)[2]
> ➤ LinkedIn Premium Business for $59.99/month (or $575.88/year)
> ➤ LinkedIn Sales Navigator Pro for $79.99/month (or $779.88/year)
> ➤ LinkedIn Sales Navigator Team for $134.99/month (or $1,240/year)
> ➤ LinkedIn Recruiter Lite for $119.99/month (or $1,199.40/year)

Note that LinkedIn does offer a discount if you pay for a year in advance, or if you buy multiple licenses (accounts).

---

2   If you're a veteran, LinkedIn offers you one year of LinkedIn Premium Career for free! socialimpact.linkedin.com/programs/veterans/premiumform

If you're considering a Premium account, use one of the offers they give you for a one-month free trial. Do keep in mind, though, that LinkedIn will require you to input a credit card to get your free month, and they will bill you if you don't cancel by the end of your free month.

If you *do* upgrade, I would go with the lowest level first and then move up based on features you need access to.

Also, make sure that you're getting value out of Premium. If not, you can cancel it at any time and add it back in again later.

I've used the Job Seeker version before, and it's helpful but I'm not sure if it's worth an ongoing investment. I've found Business Premium to be a worthy investment for me.

No, I don't make money on any referrals to upgrade to Premium, and yes, I regularly advise clients who wish to upgrade.

"But Brenda," you ask, "what do you GET with LinkedIn Business Premium?"
There are multiple features you get with Premium, but here are the ones I find most valuable:

➤ **Unlimited views of "Who's Viewed Your Profile."** This is a golden list, especially if you have an optimized profile and you are super active on LinkedIn.

I will review this list at least once a week and send a personalized invitation to those people who match my target audience criteria. I don't mention that I saw that they looked at my profile. That's awkward. Don't be awkward!

Instead, I make the invitation all about them and let them know that I looked at *their* profile.

Sometimes the person will comment back to me that they looked at my profile recently (perhaps because they didn't know if I noticed or to acknowledge that they know that I looked at their profile and in a subtle way to explain WHY they were looking at my profile, and that they also appreciated that I wasn't overly sales-y by mentioning they looked at my profile. This reminds me of that episode in friends. "But they don't KNOW that we KNOW that they KNOW...").

At any rate, do this once a week and you may be pleasantly surprised. Consider this area like a fishing pond for potential clients. You're welcome.

In addition to 2nd or 3rd level connections, you may also find 1st level connections looking at your profile. These people may be current or former clients, or potential referrals for you.

If it's been a while since you've talked with them, I recommend you send them a message. I would still NOT mention that you saw they looked at your profile. Instead, just start a light conversation and comment on their LinkedIn or business activities and let the conversation take care of itself. Even better, go to THEIR profile. Find their activity feed and comment on one of their recent posts.

I'm not a salesperson. I'm a marketer. I hate it when people sell to me in an invite, and I bet you hate it, too.

Your better approach is to be a decent, professional human being. The best professional relationships on LinkedIn are those that are developed through your personal brand over time. There are no quick hits to success.

➤ **Unlimited searches**. As a LinkedIn trainer and coach, I am frequently searching for profiles for comparisons for my clients.

I typically hit the search limit with the free version of LinkedIn early on in the month. If you do a lot of searches, the paid version of LinkedIn (Premium) is worth the price.

➤ **Live chat with LinkedIn.** This is a newer feature available to Premium members, and one that I use a few times a year when I'm experiencing a problem on LinkedIn that I can't resolve on my own. For example, this year I was helping a client with social media management and they could not access their LinkedIn company page. The person who created the page was the only admin, and he had left the company and then passed away. LinkedIn chat's support was able to provide me with links to give my clients instructions on how to regain page access.

➤ **Other Premium features.** LinkedIn provides a handful of other features to their Premium users, which you can certainly check out.

Don't get too excited about the InMail credits you receive, which give you the ability to message anyone on LinkedIn even if they aren't a connection. An InMail is a single touchpoint which may or may not be read. I'd rather connect with the person and get some dialog going (or even just have my name appear in the homepage feed and let THEM form an impression of me over time) rather than pitch them using an InMail and be ignored.

View purchase history
This is available for billing activity YTD. If you're not using any features of Premium, the total is the amount of money you have paid to LinkedIn. I don't like seeing people waste money. When in doubt, cancel at the end of your current billing cycle.

Partners & services

➤ **Microsoft**
➤ **Twitter**

Microsoft

I've never used the "Microsoft" setting, but do check this if you're not sure what this means.

Twitter settings. I only recommend you add your Twitter account to your LinkedIn profile if you're active on Twitter and if your Twitter activity supports your business and your career. Also keep in mind that you can add multiple Twitter accounts to your profile (for example: your personal Twitter account and your company Twitter account). All Twitter accounts you list will require you to enter your Twitter username and password, and then they become clickable in your contact info section.

Account management

➤ **Merge accounts**
➤ **Hibernate account**
➤ **Close account**

Merge accounts

Have you ever looked up your own name on LinkedIn? If so, you might be surprised to find that:

1. **You have duplicate accounts.** This might be because you set up an account years ago and forgot about it entirely, or forgot your login and created a new one. Whenever I'm in a coaching or team training session, I ask the participant to type in their

own name and click search results for PEOPLE. One client had *four* different accounts, and they were all hers! Yes, there's a way to consolidate and delete inactive accounts.

The main reason this is a problem is that people may be pulling up the wrong account to connect with you. Or, if they connected with your old account, they may have been trying to message you with no response from you.

2. **Someone may have created an account and is posing as you.** In this day and age of identity theft, it is a definite possibility, and until someone notices and tells you, their account connections may grow.

If you do find duplicate accounts, I recommend you delete any inactive accounts and/or notify LinkedIn. The easiest way to do this is to try to log into the old accounts and go in and delete them. If you have a bunch of connections in the inactive account, you may wish to merge accounts.

If you can't remember your login, you will need to contact LinkedIn and take a picture of the front and back of your driver's license and send it to LinkedIn. This is to ensure that the person who is requesting the account be closed is the real person.

Hibernate account

This is a newer feature that allows you to temporarily deactivate your account. I've never had to use it, but I imagine if you're taking an extended leave of absence from work for personal reasons this might be useful for you.

Close account

There are only two reasons I could see someone reading this book who is looking this up and is wondering how to close a LinkedIn account.

1. **You've discovered a duplicate account.** The easiest way is to follow the on-screen instructions to log into your old account. If you still have access to the email that you used to set up the old account, you can send yourself a password reset and then go in and delete your account. Follow the on-screen instructions to merge accounts if you have several connections in an inactive account.

2. **The person is no longer on this earth.** We leave a digital legacy and not many people leave instructions on how to access accounts. If you are reading this book and haven't included instructions in your will about accessing and/or closing your social media accounts (including LinkedIn), I recommend you do so. Or at least make sure you're connected with a spouse, partner, or family member who knows how to access your home email if the need arises.

Later in this book, I'm going to mention the notifications feature of LinkedIn. One of the notifications is for 'work anniversary.' I always make sure that I know with 100% certainty that the person is still at that employer and still on this earth before congratulating them. I once discovered through the timeline feed that a person I was connected with and didn't know well had passed away and many well-wishers were writing on his anniversary notification, congratulating him for his work anniversary.

My favorite pie is Boston Cream.
I love the creamy and fluffy stuff!
~ Roseanne Bottone
www.linkedin.com/in/roseannebottone

Chapter 9:

Sign in & Security

Grace: I thought I would cook Shepherd's Pie.
Will: Pray tell, Julia Child, what's in Shepherd's Pie?
Grace: Um... shepherds? Sheep? Pie?
~ Will & Grace, Season 1

Account access

Within "Account access" there are several links I recommend you review.

➤ **Email addresses**
➤ **Phone numbers**
➤ **Change password**
➤ **Where you're signed in**
➤ **Two-step verification**

Email addresses

Click "change" on the right side of this area to see the email addresses you have associated with your LinkedIn account. Only one email can be designated as your primary, but you can list multiple email addresses on your account.

The one you designate as primary is the email that people will see if they connect with you.

I recommend that your work email be your primary email.

WHY? LinkedIn is used primarily by people for professional networking and business purposes. Some people aren't on LinkedIn every day, and your profile visitors may want to contact you through email instead of through LinkedIn.

If I want to do business with you, I may feel funny sending an email to your AOL or Gmail box. Also, I might question your loyalty to the company if your personal email is listed rather than your work email.

"Are they thinking about leaving the company?"

"Does earthlink.net even exist anymore? That might not be a valid email."

"Why do they have "partyguy999@hotmail.com" as their contact email? That's a bit odd for a CPA. Never mind, I'm not contacting this person…"

These are just a few reactions that may occur if you use a personal email instead of your work email as your designated primary email.

If you do decide to use an email other than your work email for your primary email, just make sure it's professional (aka boring).

My personal email is mellerbrenda@gmail.com which is easy to remember and won't cause anyone to question my professionalism.

If you do decide to use a personal email, I recommend you use a "contemporary" email provider. Once upon a time, I used Hotmail as my personal email when a friend told me that using this provider made me look like I was *way* behind the times.

"They don't even make Hotmail emails anymore, do they? Doesn't make you look very progressive, does it?," Philip smirked at me as we discussed it.
www.linkedin.com/in/philipmcavoy

Yes, it hurt a little to hear it, but I'm glad Philip said so, because he was right. Hotmail *was* old and it made me look dated. One thing about the digital age: you have to appear as if you're keeping up with the times.

Keep in mind that you CAN and you SHOULD (in my opinion) have multiple email addresses linked to your LinkedIn account. If you ever have a problem accessing your primary email, you can use any of your alternate emails to access your account and to reset the password, and even change your primary email.

I once had a client who changed jobs and only had her work email listed. It took us *three hours* over the course of two weeks to get her access granted back into her account. It would have been so much easier if she had had another email listed.

The only exception to this might be if you're:

1. **Not working for an organization and you don't have a work email.** In this case, I still recommend your email is a professionally appropriate email. If you're not sure if your email is professionally appropriate, it's probably not.

2. **You're considering making a move and you don't want anyone contacting you using your work email listed on your account.** In this case, most people will use tact when contacting you, and even if you do get a contact into your work email, you can go into LinkedIn and respond through LinkedIn messaging and offer a home email or your personal cell phone to communicate through instead.

If your employer learns of emails sent to your work email asking you about other jobs (yes, they can check your work email. After all, they *own* the email box. No, it's not really ethical but yes there are employers who do this.), you could always explain that you didn't respond to it obviously because you are LOVING your job there. Then, maybe increase your job search efforts because who wants to be working for THAT kind of employer?!

Phone numbers

In this field, you can add a mobile phone number to be used in case you forget your password and don't want to reset it. I recommend using this and setting it up with your personal mobile phone (if you're fancy and have a personal phone and work cell phone; if you're a mere mortal like me, you just have one mobile phone). Note that by adding your phone number here, it does not show in your 'contact info.' More on that later.

Change password

How long has it been since you changed your LinkedIn password? If it's been more than a year, I recommend you change it. Why? Well, it's just good online behavior to periodically change your passwords.

> If your IT person or legal team was sitting next to me, they'd probably offer some fancy rationale about changing your password that would scare you into never going online again.[3]

My personal point of view is that LinkedIn is a professional networking site. You're not entering your social security number, blood type, or any

---

3   Check out this post for a few responses from IT experts and others about changing passwords: www.linkedin.com/posts/brendameller_linkedin-linkedinstrategy-password -activity-6721230908025798656-qK-T

critical financial information, but you ARE using it as a virtual Rolodex of sorts.

The higher up you go in an organization, the more likely (in my experience) you could be targeted for a security breach of your LinkedIn account. Why? Bragging rights by hackers.

I once had a client call me in a panic because his boss' account was hacked. His boss was the *president* of his company.

He asked me what to do. My advice to him? Screenshot anything they did or posted. Document what happened. Tell the boss to change their password immediately, and then determine if you need to contact your PR firm for damage control, the police (if a crime occurred while using your account), LinkedIn to notify them of the security breach, and/or anyone else who may have been impacted by the hack.

The average person on LinkedIn simply isn't an appealing enough target for the average hacker to try to access their account.

But let's not make it easy for them. Change your LinkedIn password at least once a year. Or, better yet, follow the same password change frequency they force you to do at work. Or, use their two-step verification.

Where you're signed in

This is interesting and something I'll look at every few months. I use a VPN and it sometimes scrambles my IP address, which means the locations that LinkedIn says I logged in (and didn't log out from) are really difficult to assess for validity.

A good rule of thumb: use a VPN when accessing your accounts out in public to minimize the risk that someone can see your account logins

/ passwords, and log out whenever you're using a public computer to access your LinkedIn account.

It can't hurt (and may help) if you log out of all sessions. Just know that the next time you log into LinkedIn from your laptop, desktop, or phone, it will require you to enter your password.

Devices that remember your password
I don't have this enabled on my profile, nor have I seen anyone talking about this feature yet. This is a new feature. I'll update the digital version of this book once I determine what this setting does.

Two-step verification
I recently enabled this feature since it offers an additional level of safety if your account has been hacked or if you're worried that people may be using your LinkedIn account without your knowledge or permission.

Basically, what happens here is LinkedIn sends you a verification code every time you log in from a new device. You only have to enter the code once per device.

My favorite pie is coconut cream pie!
~ Stefanie Hudson
www.linkedin.com/in/stefaniehudson

Chapter 10:

Visibility

Jack: Just get him [Tracy] back in time for the show. I have a very full plate.
Liz: Really? Is it from that pie place?
Jack: And I'm tired of going to bat for you and your show.
Liz: Oh. Ok. Fine. But just to be clear....
Jack: There is no pie!

— 30 Rock, Season 5

➤ **Visibility of your profile & network**
➤ **Visibility of your LinkedIn activity**

Visibility of your profile & network

Within this area, there are multiple items. I'll focus on the items I've found to be the most important, and I'll also tell you which ones I skip.

Profile viewing options

I recommend setting this to 'Full Profile,' which enables other people to see your name, headline, and photo if you've viewed their profile. Keep in mind that a good portion of your LinkedIn connections are using the free version of LinkedIn, so they can only see the most recent 2-3 people who have looked at their profile.

Then there are the people who have Premium access, but they may not be looking every single day.

My own experience is that people really don't pay too close attention to how often people are looking at their profiles, nor do they really care.

One person I know who has Premium and *does* pay close attention to this is Beth Granger (www.linkedin.com/in/bethgranger). I know if I look at her profile and it's been a while, she may send me a message the same or next day to say "hello."

Plus, if you look at someone's profile and they may be a good referral or potential lead but for whatever reason you don't send them an invite, they can see that you've looked at their profile, which may prompt them to visit YOUR profile and send you an invitation to connect. Yes, this has happened to me. And, yes, this has led to new business for me. People don't like to be sold to, but they do like to discover someone offering a service they need.

That said, be aware that if you have this set to **Full Profile**, people can see that you've looked at their profile. So be aware of former bosses, ex-significant others, frenemies, and competitors who may be seeing you looking at their profile. The risk is low, but there is potential for them to know.

Some of my executive clients keep this setting to anonymous instead. It's perfectly fine to do so, and it's a personal preference. And, yes, you can toggle this on and off as needed, but I don't recommend it (because you have to remember to do this…).

But you're not reading this book to find out how you can be harder to find and connect with on LinkedIn, are you? The "Full Profile" setting could bring opportunities to you without any additional effort.

I've had multiple occasions when I've visited a prospect's profile without sending them an invite, and a day or so later they send ME an invite to connect.

It's like drawing moths to a flame, I tell you.

Edit your public profile

Click this heading and it will take you a web page titled "Public profile settings." When you land on this page, you'll be able to see what other people (not connected to you) see when they view your profile.

As you navigate this page, remember "CHOOSE GREEN TO BE SEEN." Your goal is to set all areas to maximum visibility if you want to come up in more profile searches and keep people on your profile longer when they do visit. Maximum visibility may also encourage more invitations to be sent to you by these page visitors.

The action areas are on the right side of your screen, from top to bottom.

Edit your custom URL

If your LinkedIn web address (or URL) has a bunch of gobbledygook non-sense characters at the end, it needs to be cleaned up. I have no idea WHY LinkedIn does this, other than as a way to randomly assign a LinkedIn page address with a numeric identifier at the end of it.

Let's say for example that my LinkedIn URL was:

www.linkedin.com/in/brenda-meller-78298310a

Not only is this difficult to try to type in (Is there a dash here? Was that 782 or 728?), but it also signifies a LinkedIn user who is either not aware of the ability to simplify the URL. Believe me, once you know you can change this, you'll want to change it right away.

Once you simplify it, LinkedIn will take a day or two for the new URL to be indexed by Google and the other search engines, and anyone visiting your profile will see the new, cleaned up URL.

I don't recommend changing your URL frequently, as you're trying to build a brand and you want to establish trust with your page visitors using a

URL that you've chosen. But cleaning it up to remove the alpha-numeric code and make your web address INTENTIONAL is a good plan.

To change and simplify your URL, simply click on the pencil icon next to the URL. You'll then be able to edit the text that appears after the last slash mark.

I recommend you simplify your URL to remove the nonsensical alpha-numeric characters and to remove the dash between your first and last name.

So, my corrected URL is now:

www.linkedin.com/in/brendameller

Once you're happy with the new URL, click SAVE.

As long as nobody else is already using the URL, you should be all set. If, however, you have a common name and someone else has already claimed that URL, LinkedIn will give you an error message that it's not available. In this case, I recommend you add a middle initial or a keyword or abbreviation to the end.

For example:

BrendaLMeller or brendamellerMI (for Michigan)

Note that the URL is *not* case sensitive so these would be changed to:

www.linkedin.com/in/brendalmeller
www.linkedin.com/in/brendamellermi

I've also seen people add their industry or job title to the end of their URL. For example:

www.linkedin.com/in/brendamellermarketing
www.linkedin.com/in/brendamellerauthor

Your text must include a minimum of 5 but no more than 30 characters, and no spaces.[4]

Edit content
Let's skip this for now. We'll work on this in your 'profile optimization' later in this book.

Edit visibility
Remember CHOOSE GREEN TO BE SEEN.

Make sure that "Your profile's public visibility" is toggled to "Show," which makes the button area GREEN.

If you toggle it to "Off" you'll notice that nobody can see anything on your profile. Eek!

Make sure that "Basic (required)" is checked off to show your name, number of connections, and region.

Next, under "Profile photo," make sure to check the box so your photo is set to "Public," which allows everyone to see your photo– regardless of whether or not they're connected to you.

I've read that if you have a photo on your account, and if it's public, you will receive 21x more profile views[5] and receive 9x more invitation requests.[6]

---

4   www.linkedin.com/help/linkedin/answer/87/customizing-your-public-profile-url
5   blog.linkedin.com/2017/march/14/linkedin-profile-photo-tips-introducing-ph
oto-filters-and-editing
6   expandedramblings.com/index.php/by-the-numbers-a-few-important-linked
in-stats

Underneath your photo settings, there are a whole bunch of other areas: background photo, headline, etc. etc.

Everything should be set to SHOW. CHOOSE GREEN TO BE SEEN!

That's it. There is no SAVE button anywhere on this page except for the URL change, which can be a bit unnerving.

However, you may see this message pop up in the bottom left of your page:

"Success! We've updated your settings. Search engines can take some time to detect changes and refresh. LinkedIn does not control that refresh process."

Who can see or download your email address
I recommend you set this to 1st level connections. This means that only people who you choose to connect with (or accept invitations from) get to see your email address.

There is also a little button in there that allows you to make your email downloadable to people who export your connections list and, unless you're the kind of person who experiences great joy in being added to email newsletters without asking to do so, I'd leave the button gray (set to "No").

Who can see your connections
I recommend you set this to "Your connections." This helps potential future connections as they will see who you have in common when sending you an invite to connect OR when deciding whether or not to accept your invitation.

However, I have heard of C-suite executives and those in HR/recruiting roles who prefer NOT to share their connections list because they know that some people connect with them only to harvest their connections list. In that case, I would agree it makes sense to HIDE your connections.

Who can see your last name

I recommend setting this to show your FULL name, unless there's a personal reason you prefer not to show your last name. My goal for you is to help you come up in more searches and to drive profile views, and showing your full last name helps with both.

Representing your organization and interests

I recommend you set this to YES, but make sure you read the description. The way I see it is if you've added your current employer to your profile, there is an affiliation anyway.

Profile visibility off LinkedIn

I recommend this setting be set to YES so we can see your profile in Google searches, etc.

Manage who can discover your profile from your email address

For both of these areas, I set this to "Everyone" and recommend you do, too, unless you're trying to be very selective and you don't want them to find your profile, even if they have your email address or phone number.

Blocking

Visit this section to see a list of people you have blocked on LinkedIn. You can block up to 1,200 people. They won't be able to see you, and you won't be able to see them. You can learn more about the blocking feature in Chapter 14.

Visibility of your LinkedIn activity

Manage active status

I have this set to "Your connections only" and would recommend this, as I don't see any benefit to having non-connections see when I'm online.

Share job changes, education changes, and work anniversaries from profile

Once upon a time, LinkedIn had this setting for "Profile updates" and we would see *every* time someone updated their headline, photo, about, etc.

Enough people probably complained about this feature so now they limit it to just a few outgoing notifications. More on how to use these notifications later.

For now, I recommend you keep this set to YES so that a notification goes out to your network when you change jobs (or get promoted), change education, and/or celebrate a work anniversary.

Notifying connections when you're in the news

I recommend setting this to YES so that a notification automatically goes on LinkedIn when you are mentioned in an industry article that is shared on LinkedIn.

Mentions by others

I recommend setting this to YES so that others can mention (tag) you, regardless of whether or not you are connected. Here's a video showing tags: youtu.be/3egBhidZwmc

Followers

I recommend you have this set to "everyone" to allow anyone on LinkedIn to follow you. By following you, someone will be able to see your posts on LinkedIn, even if they are not connected to you. Plus, there is no approval needed to follow someone.

If you have a large network on LinkedIn and you're receiving a large number of new connection requests every day and can't keep up with them, you may wish to set "Make follow primary" to YES. By doing so, your default "Connect" button on your LinkedIn profile changes to "Follow" instead. Those people who really want to follow you will have to take the additional step of clicking the "More" button and then selecting "Personalize an invite" or "Connect" to make an official connection request.

I changed my default button to FOLLOW about a year ago and it has greatly reduced connection requests, and my follower count has increased at a steady rate. I still get a handful of invitation requests which I screen in. More on this later.

Unfortunately, changing to "Make follow primary" doesn't reduce the connection requests suggested by LinkedIn, so you will still receive "passive" connection requests from people who follow LinkedIn's suggestion to "connect" using the 'quick connect' button.

My favorite pie is blueberry, how about you?
~ Jason Gozikowski
www.linkedin.com/in/jason-gozikowski

Chapter 11:

Communications

Brenda: The special pasta today is spaghetti. It has meatballs on it, with a red sauce, um, I think it's tomato.... And for dessert we have pie. We have peach pie, cherry pie, apple pie, pecan pie, lemon pie, cream pie...honey pie. But if you want pizza pie, you gotta go across the street. Ask for Grito, he'll take care of ya. So what will it be?
— *Beverly Hills, 90210, Season 1*

I don't spend too much time in this area, other than one: birthday notifications. I also noticed LinkedIn moved a few other items in here, as explained below.

How do you get your notifications

My philosophy is that LinkedIn is a professional networking site, and I don't feel the need to see birthday notifications for people I only know professionally. If I'm friends with you on Facebook, I'll wish you a happy birthday there.

I do know some people prefer to keep this notification on, as it gives them a point of communication with people in their network. I find this especially for those in a heavy sales-focused industry, such as real estate, personal finance, mortgage companies, or similar services.

Whatever you decide to do is up to you, but if birthday notifications annoy you, you can turn them off. To do so:

➤ Select **On LinkedIn.**
➤ Click on **Network (Groups, events, anniversaries, invites, birthdays).**
➤ Toggle **Birthdays in your network** to the OFF position.

Who can reach you

Invitations to connect
I have this set to Everyone and recommend you do, too, unless you're trying to be very selective on who you add to your network. If you click this area, you'll see you can limit this to people who have your email address or people who appear in your imported contacts list.

Invitations from your network
Within this area, you can indicate if you're open to invitations from pages to follow as well as events to attend, or if you'd like to shut these off. I recommend keeping them on. You can decline page follows or event invites if they are not relevant or interesting to you.

Messages
Within this area, there are several settings. My settings are as follows:

For "Enable message request notifications," I have set this to 'Yes.'

For "Allow others to send you InMail," I have set this to 'No.' I personally find that 99% of InMails are filled with people trying to sell me something.

If they want to connect, they will typically message me or comment on a post indicating this. Or, they will email me.

For "Allow LinkedIn partners to show you sponsored messages," I have set this to 'No.' These messages might include sales messages or messages as part of a hiring campaign (aka: job leads), neither of which I'm interested in. However, you might be– especially if you're in career transition.

Research invites
I have this set to 'Yes' to allow LinkedIn to message me about research opportunities, but I often pass because they ask you to sign a non-disclosure if they are asking about new site features (and I like to talk about my experiences!).

Messaging experience

Read receipts and typing indicators
I have this shut off. I don't need to see that you've read my message or when you're typing, nor do I wish to see this of my connections.

Reply suggestions
I checked 'Yes' here so LinkedIn offers me some pre-populated reply suggestions, which I occasionally use. But not always! I want people to know I'm a real person, not a bot!

> *Brenda, I'll start this invitation request with my favorite pie: Mom's lemon meringue. (She passed away decades ago and nothing touches the memory.)*
> *~ Collier Ward*
> *www.linkedin.com/in/collier1960*

Chapter 12:

Data Privacy

"So learn about life. Cut yourself a big slice
with the silver server, a big slice of pie.
Open your eyes. Let life happen."

~ *Sylvia Plath*

How LinkedIn uses your data

I don't spend a lot of time in this area, but feel free to poke around each of the settings in this area if you're curious about the information. My personal philosophy is that I don't mind that LinkedIn is using my data. I'm not putting anything overly personal, or sharing sensitive or private information on the site. Sure, you could spend time poring through every setting here, but what's the gain for that time you spend?

Personally, the only setting I look at in this area is '**Get a copy of your data.**'

The one thing I will do is export a copy of my connections list once or twice a year. *Why?*

1. Because LinkedIn allows any user to do this for their connections list right now. It's not a Premium-only feature– yet. (But my guess is it *could* be in the future.)

2. Because if LinkedIn ever goes away, I know I have a copy of my connections list. Many of us are using LinkedIn as a replacement for a Rolodex (remember those?).

3. Because when I export my connections list, I can review it and sort/search using Excel, which I find a bit easier than LinkedIn search.

I recommend these steps. First, click to go into this menu. Then, under "Want something in particular? Select the data files you are most interested in," select "Connections." At this point, LinkedIn will ask you to input your password and it will take about ten minutes or so for the data to be ready to download.

Once it's done, you'll receive an email from LinkedIn titled: "Your LinkedIn data archive is ready!" stating that your data is ready to download. You'll have to click the link to return to this area in 'Privacy' to download the data.

From there, you will have a .CSV file that you can save on your desktop for reference, and you can then format and work with the data as you see fit.

Once upon a time, the data would contain email addresses for all your connections. I think too many people were using this feature to scrape the emails and add people to their newsletters.

This is a big no-no for a mass email list. Technically, you are supposed to obtain permission from people before adding them to your email list. By accepting a connection request, you are *not* asking for their email.

Side note: If you are one of those people who adds every connection to your email newsletter, please stop. If we wanted your email newsletter, we would ask for it. It's like scooping out a huge slice of banana cream pie and dropping it on our plates at Thanksgiving when we are full and don't want another bite.

Then, we have two choices: be polite and take a small bite or two so as not to offend the host, or decline the pie which then has to be discarded or put aside for the next day. And when we DO eat the pie, we are remembering how it was served to us without our permission and we're a bit irritated all over again.

Don't force pie on people! Pie should always be *appreciated*.

Anyway, back to your exported data file. The fields in the file include: First Name, Last Name, Email Address (only if the person has selected to share it in the export), Company, Position (current position, not the same as headline), and Connected On (the date you connected with this person).

It's not a complete list of all your connection data, but it gives you enough if you are trying to find that woman Michelle you met at a networking event a month or so ago.

Or perhaps you are reviewing your connections for specific job titles or companies. At any rate, the data is yours to sort and manipulate as needed, and you can always add in additional columns with notes or use the data in other ways.

Just make sure you're not spamming everyone with your email newsletter.

Remember: *not everybody is hungry for banana cream pie.*

Job seeking preferences
If you're considering making a career move in the next year or so, or if you're actively in career transition now, make sure you look at every area in this section.

Job application settings

This is the only place I would ever upload a copy of my resume on LinkedIn, except if I were applying for a job.

Sharing your profile when you click 'Apply'

If you are a job seeker, I recommend you change this to 'Yes.'

Commute preferences

Review and fill out your preferences.

Signal your interest to recruiters at companies you've created job alerts for

If you are a job seeker, I recommend you change this to 'Yes.'

Stored job applicant accounts

If you are a job seeker, I recommend you review this list, and remove anything that looks unfamiliar to you.

One More Thing: #OPENTOWORK

LinkedIn used to make the feature called "Let recruiters know you're open to opportunities" easy to find here, but now it's on your profile.

If I were you? I'd go to your profile and add /opportunities/job-opportunities/edit/ to the end of your LinkedIn URL, so it reads something like this:

www.linkedin.com/in/brendameller/opportunities/job-opport
unities/edit/

I recommend filling this out completely if you want to come up in more searches by recruiters.

Note here that LinkedIn says, "We take steps to not show recruiters at your current company, though can't guarantee complete privacy."

What this means is if you work for ABC Company and the person responsible for hiring at your company has the paid recruiter version of LinkedIn, they won't show your profile to that recruiter.

However, let's say your company outsources its recruiting to XYZ Agency. Well then that recruiter COULD see that you're open. Also, recruiters talk and could share information with each other. So, proceed with caution.

My personal philosophy is that you are ultimately in charge of your career. So even if you get caught with this setting on, you could explain to your employer that you either didn't realize the setting was enabled or you aren't actively seeking– but any smart person should always be open to career conversations unless their current employer is guaranteeing them employment for the rest of their career.

Most companies won't spend a lot of time reviewing this to see which of their employees are 'open' but some might; weigh the risk against the benefits.

I have heard that when you have your profile set to 'open to work,' your profile will come up in more searches by recruiters and if you do apply to a job at their company, your name goes into a separate category (smaller list) than the general pool of LinkedIn candidates, thereby increasing your attractiveness as a candidate.

Be careful though– if you select to show to 'All LinkedIn members' that you are looking for a new opportunity, LinkedIn adds a green frame around your headshot photo circle that reads: #OPENTOWORK.

If you're unemployed and actively seeking your next role, this could give you added visibility. But if you're working and trying to *quietly* find job opportunities, do NOT choose to show to "All LinkedIn members." You could, however, designate to show this to 'Recruiters only.'

Personally, I'm not a fan of the green frame indicating you're open to work because it seems too obvious, like a neon flashing sign. But that's my opinion as a marketer.

Other applications

Permitted services
I recommend you review this list, and remove anything that looks unfamiliar to you.

Microsoft Word
If you're a job seeker, you may want to keep this on YES to make a copy of your profile easily downloadable in Word format. Otherwise, I turn this feature off (set to NO).

My favorite pie, (besides #SocialMediaPie) would be
(Michigan) Cherry Pie with crumble topping.
~ Phil Samuels
www.linkedin.com/in/philsamuels

Chapter 13:

Advertising Data

"I know that I am essentially a sort of fun-loving person who really just wants to sit around and eat pies."
~ *Nora Ephron*

I spend no time looking around the advertising data section, but feel free to look through your ad settings if you don't like the ads being served to you on LinkedIn. My point of view is that LinkedIn is a business and they have to make money. I'm fine with ads being shown to me, but very rarely do I ever click on them.

I do think that ads on LinkedIn can be an effective marketing tool but only if you have an optimized profile and company page, if your sales team is active on LinkedIn (and practices good invitation strategy and generates network engagement), and if you are super focused on your target audience.

You can screen out people who don't need to see your ads. For example, at least once a week I see ads for master's degrees in my homepage feed as "sponsored posts" which means they are ads. I have a dual MBA / MS in marketing. I have zero desire of ever returning for another master's degree; the organization targeting those ads to me is wasting money. They either don't know that you can target to EXCLUDE people with a master's degree, or they simply don't understand advertising.

By the way, if you need help with LinkedIn ads, I highly recommend AJ Wilcox (www.linkedin.com/in/wilcoxaj). His company specializes in LinkedIn ad management for their clients. No, I don't earn a referral fee for sending him business. I just think he's brilliant. I've learned a lot about LinkedIn ad best practices from him.

My favorite pie is Key Lime!
~ Emma Pietroleonardo
www.linkedin.com/in/emma-pietroleonardo

Chapter 14:

Unfollowing, Disconnecting, Reporting, and Blocking

Larry: Grape works as a soda. Sort of as a gum. I wonder why it doesn't work as a pie. Grape pie? There's no grape pie.
~ Curb Your Enthusiasm, Season 2

You may connect with some people on LinkedIn that you later regret connecting with. Or, perhaps their network activity isn't appealing to you, or it annoys you.

Or, maybe you connected when you were working with each other, and you no longer wish to see their updates but you don't want to push them out of your professional network entirely.

Or, maybe the circumstances of your personal or professional relationship would make it awkward to decline their invitation to connect, but you have ZERO desire to see their updates and activity in your homepage feed.

I'm not here to judge. I'm here to provide you answers. So, let's review the ways to see people less often in your homepage feed and on LinkedIn: unfollowing, disconnecting, reporting, and blocking.

Unfollowing

When you connect with someone on LinkedIn, you are automatically following their updates. This means any time they post on LinkedIn, you have the potential of seeing their updates and activity in your LinkedIn homepage feed.

If their content is not getting a lot of engagement or if they rarely post, you won't see them at all.

You can also FOLLOW someone on LinkedIn without connecting with them. Some people (myself included) have changed their default profile action button from CONNECT to FOLLOW to encourage people to *follow* their updates.

They may do this because they are very selective about who they connect with.

They may do this because they are getting so many new connection requests in each day, they can't keep up with them.

They may do this because they are finding that invitations tend to be more passive than intentional. This is usually the case when people send an invitation to connect based on LinkedIn's suggested connection list, and they randomly click CONNECT on ten profiles at a time.

There is a maximum connection limit on LinkedIn of 30,000 people. Once you reach this limit, you are no longer able to accept new invitation requests. You would have to disconnect from someone to create space to accept a new connection.

However, there is no current cap for *followers*. Therefore, if you have over 15,000 connections, I recommend you start being a bit more selective about whose invitations you accept. Otherwise, you're going to quickly find yourself in a situation with 30,000 connections, unable to add quality connections to your network, thereby forcing you to disconnect from people who aren't a fit.

Back to you and *unfollowing*. If you wish to unfollow someone, you can do so by clicking on the three dots in the upper right-hand corner of the post and click "Unfollow [first name]."

What I like about this is that you don't have to visit their profile, so it minimizes the chance that they are going to notice your name coming up in the "Who's viewed your profile" list.

You can also go to their profile and click the "MORE" button and then "Unfollow."

The person will NOT get a notification indicating you've unfollowed them. And, honestly, they probably will not even notice it at all. It's a pretty simple technique if you want to stay connected, but stop seeing so many of their posts and activities (likes, comments) because they aren't valuable to you.

Disconnecting (Remove Connection)

Disconnecting is a further step away from that connection than unfollowing.

Disconnecting from someone on LinkedIn is something I don't do often, and only when the person does some activity that doesn't align with my values or how I'm using LinkedIn. When you disconnect from a person, they will no longer be able to see your shared connections or any other information on your profile that is not public.

They will also see fewer posts from you in their homepage feed, unless you have several common connections and you are very active and have a strong presence on LinkedIn.

The great thing is that when you disconnect from a person on LinkedIn, they don't get a notification. The only way they would know is by visiting your profile; they would now see the "1st" connection change to "2nd" or something else.

***Why disconnect and remove a connection?* Here are a few reasons why I disconnect from someone:**

1. They only seem to comment on posts from beautiful women, and they completely creep me out. This is *not* eHarmony.

2. They are overly aggressive salespeople who don't take a hint. Or, they push multiple sales messages to me via messaging, InMail, my email box, or subscribe me to their eNews without my consent.

3. We no longer work with each other and I have no desire to continue to keep in touch. I don't disconnect from my former coworkers unless my values of respect, teamwork, leadership, authority, or morals are clearly not in-sync with who they are as a person. Most former coworkers don't fall into this category for me and I stay connected.

4. They post a negative comment about me or someone I greatly respect on a post. I don't do this for every negative comment, but if it's clear we no longer have mutual respect, I disconnect. I choose to surround myself and connect with only those who align with my values.

5. They appear to be a fake account or spam. Sometimes I'm alerted of this by shared connections.

There may be a few other reasons, but these cover the majority of disconnects I've made in the past.

I've had a few people ask if they should periodically reduce their connections list by disconnecting with people they've never interacted with. My response, not unless they've done something to prompt you to disconnect. You never know where the future may lead and when a random connection can refer business or an opportunity to you, or be a connection to help you make a connection at a targeted organization.

Reporting

Very rarely, you'll have an encounter with a connection on a post or in an invitation that is unprofessional, inappropriate, threatening, or otherwise spammy. When this happens, I recommend you report them to LinkedIn.

Reporting people to LinkedIn shifts the responsibility to LinkedIn, and also helps the rest of us.

How?

Well, unsavory people on LinkedIn are like weeds in a garden. They're going to be there. And if allowed to grow, they'll get bigger and bigger. But if you pull the weed, it stops it from growing.

If you report someone to LinkedIn, they will research the issue and ban the person from LinkedIn if they are, in fact, being inappropriate in their use of this professional network.

To report a connection to LinkedIn, go to their profile, click the MORE button, and select 'Report/Block.' I typically report first, then block.

Reporting helps to alert LinkedIn about this person.

Blocking helps me, because it prevents them from seeing my profile. More on this in a minute.

To report a person who has messaged you (but is not a connection), open the message in the desktop version of LinkedIn. In the upper right-side corner of the message, click the three dots. Then, click "Report."

Blocking

When you block someone on LinkedIn, they can no longer see your profile and you can no longer see their profile. If you search for the person, it will show a result of: "no results found."

It's not a perfect solution, as the person could view your profile by using someone else's account OR by creating a second (fake) account, but at least you are creating a hurdle.

There are levels of being connected to or accessible by people on LinkedIn, and I recommend that you only block people on LinkedIn if they give you a compelling reason to do so.

My reasons for blocking someone may include:

1. **They are creepy and they act as though LinkedIn is a dating website.** If you are approached by a creep, please report and block them. This gets them removed from LinkedIn if LinkedIn confirms they are using the site inappropriately. By ignoring the invite, they can continue their bad behavior on others. It's like weeding the garden. It doesn't prevent more weeds from growing, but it DOES stop the weeds that you see.

2. **They are an overly aggressive salesperson who does not take NO for an answer.** I don't block the typical salesperson. I understand this is a business networking site and you need to do business. But when you add me to your newsletter and then start to fill my InMail box daily with a pitch about your

business, I will first disconnect from you and, if it continues, I will block you.

3. **They act disrespectful or extremely unprofessional.** Sometimes people don't agree with me and I understand and appreciate this. However, when you attack me either in my posts or in messages and you don't seem open to a respectful dialog, I will block you. I truly do believe that people are good and should be treated with decency and respect. I don't have the time or energy to deal with trolls. This helps both of us, really.

You may have other categories for blocking people. For example, ex-spouses / significant others, former bosses or coworkers, estranged family members, people who don't like pie, or others. It's up to you to decide.

You can always review those you have blocked, and you can unblock if you change your mind later.

It's chocolate pecan. My Mother-in-Law, who's no longer with us, always made it for me.
~ E. Ray Jackson
www.linkedin.com/in/erjacksoncpa

Section 3:

Profile Optimization

Chapter 15:

How to Optimize Your LinkedIn Profile

"If you wish to make an apple pie from scratch,
you must first invent the universe."
~ Carl Sagan

An optimized profile is one that is complete, accurate, and has been created with a goal and target audience in mind. It is focused and interesting.

Why is an optimized profile so important? Your profile is your personal selling tool. Whether you are self-employed, work for a company, or you're looking for your next dream job, your profile can help you to sell your products and services– or yourself.

An optimized profile will increase your chances of being found on LinkedIn, and thereby increase the visibility of your personal brand.

It will also create visual interest for your ideal target audience when they visit your profile, which keeps them reading more.

As you are working to optimize your profile, I recommend you work on your profile updates in the desktop version of LinkedIn, and check the mobile view of your profile on the LinkedIn app along the way. Nowadays, about half of website visits occur on a mobile device, so you want to be sure to optimize your profile for both desktop and mobile views.

Keep in mind that my LinkedIn desktop view may vary slightly from your view, so some items may appear differently than what I describe in this book. Plus, LinkedIn is changing all the time, so there may be newer features on LinkedIn.com that aren't referenced in this book. Hey, I try my best! But I am an observer and I don't make the rules. That's why it's important to follow me on LinkedIn. I'll fill you in on the changes as I discover them.

Even when – *not if!* – LinkedIn does make changes, my expectation is that the changes will be gradual and not a complete overhaul. Plus, the concepts described here apply to help you understand both the technical impact as well as the marketing impact of profile optimization.

Optimize your LinkedIn profile: *be a sculptor*
When you think about optimizing your LinkedIn profile, I want you to imagine yourself as a sculptor who has just been given a giant block of marble. If you want people to look at, and admire your work of art, you have to do some sculpting.

An optimized LinkedIn profile should remind you of a sculpture. It's as much about what you take OUT as what you keep IN.

> SCULPT your online brand:
>
> ➤ Write it for your IDEAL target audience.
> ➤ Fill out every area and maximize all characters and fields.
> ➤ Write it for a person AND write it for a computer.

Now, let's expand on each of these points.

Write it for your IDEAL target audience.

First, your LinkedIn profile should be written for your ideal target audience. You are not creating your profile for every single one of LinkedIn's 722 million+ members. Instead, you are creating your profile for your *ideal target audience*. You will be keeping this in mind for every area of your LinkedIn profile.

Write down your ideal target audience. Include as much detail as you can. Sample categories may include:

➤ Job title
➤ Age
➤ Gender
➤ Geographic area(s)
➤ Company type / industry
➤ Sales revenue
➤ Number of employees

For example, my criteria may include:

➤ VP or Director of Marketing, Business Development, or Sales
➤ Attended Central Michigan University
➤ Growing Industry
➤ 10+ employees
➤ B2B
➤ Company is based in Metro Detroit
➤ Company page has over 100 followers but no content or incomplete content
➤ Profile is mostly complete but missing some key elements (no branded header, for example)

I can also include gender, age, company revenue, industry, etc. The more specific, the better.

If you haven't defined your target audience or you're not sure, think about your best (top) customers. What qualities do they share? Make sure you write something down, because this is going to help you as you create or edit your profile.

Fill out every area and maximize all characters and fields.

Look at my LinkedIn profile right now:

www.linkedin.com/in/brendameller

It contains a LOT of stuff, right? That's intentional on my part. I know that if I want to come up in more searches on LinkedIn, I have a better chance of appearing in those searches if I have filled out my profile.

I pay close attention to character limits in each area of my profile, and I consider what is viewable before my audience has to click "show more," and the difference between what they see on mobile view versus desktop view. More on this later.

For now, I would recommend you look at your profile along with these character limits. You will refer back to these later as you work through your profile.

Does that feel like I'm asking a lot? It might. But you didn't buy this book for me to tell you how wonderful you are and how perfect your profile is today. You bought this because you want to be BETTER at LinkedIn.

I'm going to deliver a lot of tough love to you throughout this book, but remember: my goal is to help you.

Know the character limits

LinkedIn sets character limits to a variety of fields within your profile. For the purposes of this book, I've listed out the most important for profile optimization (as of this writing!).

Name: First name is a maximum of 20 characters and last name is a maximum of 40 characters.

Headline: LinkedIn allows you up to 220 total characters in your headline field, but only about 80-90 characters are viewable in the desktop search results. The headline field used to be 120 characters, and in the middle of 2020, they quietly rolled out the new limit of 220.

About (previously called 'Summary'): You have 2,600 characters.

Experience: You have 2,000 characters for each position.

Skills: You can (and *should*) list up to 50 but note that only the top 3 are viewable.

Review your profile periodically

Your profile will NOT stay optimized over time. Your audience and LinkedIn prefer fresh and relevant content, so make it a point to review your profile at least once a quarter, making modifications along the way.

Feel free to visit my profile as often as you'd like as you're working on your profile updates. I always tell people two things:

1. **LinkedIn is what I specialize in for a living.** Therefore, I want to make sure I'm staying on top of LinkedIn features to maximize my profile's visibility and share this information with my clients. My goal is to help YOU look better, and my profile will always incorporate the latest techniques I'm learning. If you want an expert in accounting, you find a CPA. If you are having a medical

issue, you see a doctor. If you need help with LinkedIn, look at someone who is succeeding on the platform.

2. **When you look at my profile, it's not stalking– it's research.** LinkedIn is a professional networking site and I'm giving you permission to look at my profile. Actually, it's a step beyond that; I'm ASKING that you look at my profile. I guarantee you will learn techniques that will inspire and educate you. When I see people I know looking at my profile, I am flattered. I know they are doing their homework and that they want to improve their LinkedIn efforts.

My favorite pie… not because I love it but because my mom did. She would always try to get me to eat strawberry-rhubarb pie. Yuck!
~ Delano McGregor
www.linkedin.com/in/delano-mcgregor-mba

Chapter 16:

Your Header Image

"You like pie? I like pie."
~ Barack Obama

Can I let you in on a little secret? It's so simple that once I tell you, you won't be able to unsee it.

> *LinkedIn gives you a FREE billboard on your profile. Yes, free.*

Your LinkedIn header is the equivalent of a billboard you see on the side of the highway, and it's on every single person's LinkedIn account.

About half of the profiles I review on LinkedIn have the default header: teal green with the interconnected dots and lines.

Think about the last time you drove by a highway billboard that said: "THIS SPACE AVAILABLE." If you have the default header on your profile, you're essentially saying the same thing.

Look at your profile right now. Do you have the teal blue dots/lines default image (or the newer pastel green landscape image)?

If so... YOU ARE WASTING AN OPPORTUNITY!

> **TIP:** Change the default image NOW to something INTER-ESTING that aligns with your professional brand or your company's brand.

Your header image can fall into one of three categories:

1. **The Branded Header (my personal preference)**
   A branded header is one that supports or promotes your company, organization, or area of expertise. This image may include a photo of your company, your company logo, your company tagline, brand elements (colors, typography, photos), or other items that support your company and/or brand.

   Examples:

   Howard Davis (www.linkedin.com/in/howarddavismi) showcases client projects in his header.

   David Bann (www.linkedin.com/in/davebann) features a leader dog and a puppy. *And who doesn't love puppies?*

   Chris Meller (www.linkedin.com/in/chrismeller67) is active in networking and college recruiting. And, *yes*, he's my husband and yes, I created the header for him.

   Greg Coyne (www.linkedin.com/in/gregcoyne) uses a branded image with his website.

   Craig Fry (www.linkedin.com/in/craigfry) illustrates his product with an eye-catching brand-color background.

   Brenda Meller (yes, that's me! www.linkedin.com/in/brendameller) If you visit my profile right now and then again next month, you'll notice my header image has changed. That's intentional, as I want to create interest in this portion of my profile to drive new viewers. You will notice that I frequently use a jewel-tone color block with a dominant use of my brand color: bright magenta pink.

2. **A Geographical Header**
You may decide to use an image that nods to the geographical area in which you live, work, or do business. High-quality stock photos of city skylines to demonstrate your pride in your hometown and also provides visitors imagery that creates an immediate, familiar connection. Here are some of my favorites:

Rita Fields (www.linkedin.com/in/drritafields) is an amazing leader and inspirational speaker based in metro Detroit. I have seen several of her keynotes and she always amazes me with her insights, her humor, and her storytelling approach.

Colin Moynahan (www.linkedin.com/in/colin-moynahan) provides financial planning strategy services for millennials, and he is based in Charleston, South Carolina.

Jenna Lloyd (www.linkedin.com/in/jenna-lloyd-94a32416) works in New York City. This quickly created an emotional reaction for me. How about you?

3. **A Stock Photo Header, or Personal Interest Header**
From mountains to cool color effects, these headers could include anything that showcases a personal interest, hobby, or just something you love. Below are some of my favorite folks who have these types of profile headers:

Amanda Holdan-Sinisi (www.linkedin.com/in/aholdan-sinisi) uses an image of a mountain. She is a high achiever who enjoys a challenge.

MiVida Burrus (www.linkedin.com/in/mmburrus) uses a cool image that uniquely complements her company's brand.

Tanya Abreu (www.linkedin.com/in/tanyaabreu) has a cool bubble rainbow effect. It reminds me of a garden globe!

Pam Majchrzak (www.linkedin.com/in/pamelamajchrzak) has a visually interesting, colorful image that makes me think of patterns and energy.

These are just a few of the many LinkedIn header images I frequently cite during training sessions. I'm always on the lookout for other images, so if you have an interesting one I should check out, let me know by messaging me on LinkedIn!

Now that you have a few options to consider for your header image, how do you actually *create* your header image?

First of all, determine what type of image you want to use, and know that the image you put up now can always be changed later. In fact, I recommend you change it at least a few times a year.

Next, keep in mind the ideal image size for your LinkedIn header image is 1584 x 396 pixels. I use Canva.com to create images that are perfectly sized to these dimensions, and I export them in a .png format to upload to LinkedIn. If you have a graphic designer doing this for you, make sure you give them the proper dimensions.

Keep in mind though that your headshot photo will be in the lower left-hand corner of your header image, so don't put anything important (text, etc.) in that area.

When you're ready, you can simply upload an image to your LinkedIn header by finding a picture from your marketing department or a stock image website. I recommend Pexels.com or Unsplash.com, both of which offer free photos for unlimited and free use.

Be sure that you check the alignment by viewing your profile from the desktop version of LinkedIn as well as the mobile view. You may find that something that works well on desktop has important elements (YOUR LOGO, for example...) that are hidden on mobile. I created and use this template to guide me into the areas that are hidden by my profile photo on desktop and mobile.

The bonus when creating this LinkedIn header image in Canva is that you can create a message to lay on top of the image, as I commonly do on my header image.

Just like a billboard gets boring and then becomes virtually invisible after you've driven past it every day for a month, people start to ignore your header image if you never change it. I change my header image every month with a new marketing tip, LinkedIn tip, or product/service I am highlighting.

So, that answers the WHAT question. Now, some of you may be wondering HOW to change it. First of all, you're not alone. I've created a short video to show you how to change your LinkedIn header image: youtu.be/AY9lIsywvVo

I'd say my favorite pie is apple, with ice cream of course.
~ Monique St. Paul
www.linkedin.com/in/mstpaul

Chapter 17:

Your LinkedIn Headline

"Humility means you're willing to give someone
a bigger slice of the pie."
~ *Frederick Lenz*

If you're an experienced LinkedIn member, you know that there are many areas on your LinkedIn profile that have character limits. In MOST cases, I advise my clients to use every available character but, as in the case of your LinkedIn Headline, **where** those characters appear also matters.

Until recently, LinkedIn allowed up to just 120 characters in your headline. Now, you can have up to 220 characters.

By default, your headline is your job title at your current employer.

That's great, right? Well, not exactly.

Your key to LinkedIn success is **how you differentiate yourself** and how well you **connect with your target audience**.

One expression I use is: "people are lazy."

I really don't think that people using LinkedIn are *lazy*, but this statement will help you to remember that most people don't want to take the time to click to view your profile, or click to "see more" on sections of your profile as this disrupts their LinkedIn viewing activity.

People won't click to navigate away from their activity unless:

➤ **You give them a compelling reason to click,**

AND

➤ **They are interested in what you have to say.**

Sure, there are many people who click around on LinkedIn as they are navigating and learning the site. They may be curious as they stumble upon your profile, and decide to click on a few areas. But these people aren't usually the connections that become clients or employers.

The ones who become clients or employers are those who saw something on your profile that appealed to them.

So, let's consider your 220-character (or less) headline. If I kept mine with the default "Marketing Consultant at Meller Marketing," this would be the only text someone would see next to my name in search results.

You cannot pull up your own profile in a LinkedIn search, but you CAN search for your competition who shares your job title or other keywords.

I recommend you do a search right now for your job title or your top keywords.

What do you notice when scanning down the list? Chances are, you notice the headshot photo (or lack thereof), and things that are different, right?

The problem is that, on LinkedIn, most people keep the default "job title at current employer."

Everyone blends in, and nobody stands out.

I recommend you stand out. Obviously, you agree. Otherwise, why did you buy this book? Surely not just because you're a huge fan of mine and you support everything I do. Ok, maybe that applies for a *few* of you, but even then, are you really going to read a whole book that adds no value to you? NO, of course not. You're busy.

Just like knowing that you will only eat the whole slice of pie if the first bite is good, I know that you'll only read this whole book from cover to cover if you think it's going to help you.

(I know some of you are challenging that last statement in your head. You'll eat the whole slice of pie even if it's mediocre. But what if the crust is burnt or doughy? Or what if the filling tastes rancid or overly salty? HA. GOTCHA.)

Now that we both agree you want to stand out, let's make that happen.

Stop reading right now and open your LinkedIn. You can do this on your phone or on your desktop.

Pull up the search bar. Type in your job title. Click to see results. What do you notice? Keep in mind that you won't appear in your own search results, so don't look for yourself.

But also keep in mind that this is an example of what your audience sees when they search for those same words.

Scroll down the list and pay special attention to any headlines that are different, intriguing, and memorable.

Your goal with your LinkedIn headline is to make yourself stand out in search results, and to get people to click and GO TO *YOUR* PROFILE. That's where the magic happens, because your profile is for SELLING.

I revamped my headline to lead with what I can do and who I can help. The result since I've made this change? I receive 2-3 new inquiries *each week* asking about my services. Now, keep in mind this is what I do for a living and the change in the headline in and of itself isn't the ONLY reason for this steady stream of inquiries. But my headline certainly helps!

However, a strong headline alone won't make you successful using LinkedIn. I've been very active on LinkedIn for over a decade, and I use techniques like frequent posts and engaging with my network to keep my name top of mind, but I am certain that the headline has been part of the reason for the increase in inquiries.

Now, let's move onto headline length and take a look at my full headline:

I Help You Unlock the Power of LinkedIn | Read My Profile for LinkedIn Strategy Tips | Virtual Speaker | Team Training | Creator of #LinkedinROCK-STARS List | FYI: Headlines Can Now Have 220 Characters | Pie Enthusiast

Keep in mind, your headline is not completely visible to everyone.

Consider this: when you appear in search results, LinkedIn cuts off your headline so that only a portion of your headline is viewable. For this reason, I focus on the first 60-80 characters and advise my clients to do the same.

That said, I also use all 220 characters, because the headline is such a highly visible field. I recommend you maximize your headline by putting in keywords or phrases in descending order of importance (most important words first).

Your headline follows you around on LinkedIn (aka what appears when you respond to a post):

I decided to take this a step further, and look at how much of my headline appears when I respond to someone else's post. Here's what I noticed:

- ➤ 69 characters of my headline appeared in desktop view
- ➤ 46 characters of my headline appeared in mobile view
- ➤ My full headline at the time was 118 characters

So, what does this mean for you?

- ➤ **Unless people are clicking to view your LinkedIn profile, the most important words in your headline aren't the last few words.** The first 40-80 characters are going to get the *greatest visibility,* depending on your level of LinkedIn activity and how you interact with your network.

- ➤ **That said, you can and *should* consider using as many of the 220 characters as possible,** keeping in mind that people who are viewing those last few words are those who are ON your LinkedIn profile.

- ➤ **Your headline cuts off in different ways, depending on where it appears in LinkedIn, and the type of device used** by the viewer.

- ➤ **Keeping your LinkedIn headline as the default** (current position at current employer) may cause you to blend in with others and you'll risk losing profile views, connection requests, and other opportunities you may be seeking.

You may have noticed that my headline appears in different ways throughout this book. That's because I change my headline every few months, tweaking a word here and there as I evolve to tell my story in more focused ways to new audiences.

I have found this technique helpful in bringing me up in more search results on LinkedIn. Give it a try, and change your headline every now and again to see if you come up in more search results.

And one last tip here: make sure you SAVE your headline in a Word document, or email it to yourself. Far too often I hear from LinkedIn connections who change jobs and accidentally check the box to update their headline with their NEW job title, without realizing it overwrites their headline (which, once changed, is lost forever!).

My favorite pie is a carrot pie.
~ Aleksander Machel
www.linkedin.com/in/aleksandermachel

Chapter 18:

Your Headshot Photo

"If you think of life as like a big pie, you can try to hold the whole pie and kill yourself trying to keep it, or you can slice it up and give some to the people around you, and you still have plenty left for yourself."

~ Jay Leno

Your LinkedIn headshot (aka profile photo) is one of the single most important elements of your LinkedIn profile. You are setting the tone and image for your profile with this single photo, and there are several ways you can optimize your LinkedIn photo.

Use a PROFESSIONAL photo.

Yes, it's *that* important. This is the photo people will see every time you post, comment, like, or share something on LinkedIn. This is what people will see every time they visit your profile. In my experience, a professional headshot is worth the money spent. You get what you pay for, and an experienced headshot photographer will make you look your personal best on camera.

Your photo can set a positive or negative first impression. If you have taken the time to invest in a website, marketing materials, and fancy business cards, and people see a poorly lit or amateurish photo on your LinkedIn, it sends a message about your level of professionalism.

If you're an executive and you have a selfie as your headshot photo, it could make your audience question your expertise.

You could certainly have a family member or friend take a photo for you using your phone, but if you do so, make sure that it's well-lit, that you are in professional attire, and that your hair (and makeup for ladies) is done and looking fresh.

Your photo should be you at your professional *best*. It may not be exactly what you look like every day (working moms with the mom-buns, you know what I mean, right?), but it should look like you, and the absolute best professional representation of you. Whenever I have a photoshoot, I make sure it's in the morning when I feel fresh and not overly tired from a long day.

Consider your attire.

I recommend you change your photo every time your career shifts. Once upon a time, I worked in corporate America and I had a new headshot photo taken every year in a new suit: a gray suit, a navy suit, a black suit. I would change my hair color, the color of the blouse under the suit, and my accessories, but the photo was essentially the same.

When I decided to pursue a path as an independent consultant, I purged my wardrobe of just about every suit. I incorporated my brand color – pink – into about half of every outfit I wore, and every other outfit had a pop of color or some other element of fun. I had shed my corporate skin and, in doing so, I had outgrown my headshot photo.

When I went to a headshot photo session with Scott Lawrence, a local professional photographer in Metro Detroit, I brought several outfits with me that made me feel my best, and several of which incorporated my pink brand color.

Scott helped me to pick colors that would look best on camera.

On the note of color, I also recommend you invest in a personal brand and color consultation at some point in your career. I met with Patty Buccellato (www.linkedin.com/in/pattybuccellato) in 2013 for a color consultation, and it totally transformed the way I looked at colors I wore for work.

I left the appointment with my custom color wheel and a spring in my step. In the weeks immediately following this appointment, I made wardrobe changes and noticed the impact it made in my overall confidence about what I wore. Over the years, I have received so many compliments on the new color combinations I learned from Patty. The consultation was time well-spent toward a wardrobe that made me look and feel my best.[7]

Make your photo background clean and intentional.

LinkedIn is a professional networking site. It's not for *social* networking. Do not use a selfie for your photo. Do not take your LinkedIn photo in your car (yes, we can see your back seat!).

Outdoor photos are OK if the photo was captured for the purpose of a headshot, but not if you're wearing a tuxedo at your buddy's wedding or a sexy dress at a black-tie event. And, *please*, no kitchen photos with grandma's old wallpaper behind you.

Ideally, you should be staging what's in the background, if *anything* at all is in the background. Sure, a strategically placed logo or stack of bookshelves can be perfect, but only if the focal point is you. Even better is a light- or neutral-colored background.

---

7   You can read more about this appointment, her process, and my amazing results on my blog at: mellermarketing.blogspot.com/2013/07/social-media-colors-and-my -awesome.html

Your profile photo should be YOU and only you.

It should not be a group photo. It should not be with your significant other, or with you and your kids. Your photo should not be your company logo in place of a personal photo. Your photo should not be a team photo, nor should it be an illustration or a clever graphic.

I once delivered a LinkedIn team training session where several men in the room had headshot photos that included their wives. I asked them why, and they explained that they didn't want people to think they were using LinkedIn for any other reason than professional purposes, and by including their wives, it sent a very *married* message.

I replied by saying LinkedIn is a *professional* networking site. It's not eHarmony. It's not a dating site. There may be the occasional person who is thinking otherwise (more on this later), but the average person is using LinkedIn for *business* purposes. You aren't bringing your wife or spouse with you to company sales presentations, are you? If it's not an issue at those events, why would it be an issue for online networking?

Skip the spouse and focus on you– only you.

Make sure your professional appearance (shirt, top, makeup, hair) is at your personal best.

Your goal is to make a positive first impression, not to distract. Take it at a time of day when you are at your best. Ladies: please don't show a lot of skin/cleavage. It's distracting and makes us focus on your skin and not YOU as a business professional.

On this note, I think it's important to feel beautiful, but I don't feel the need to show some skin to get anyone's attention. I want my clients to hire me for my intelligence and my expertise.

I have heard that in some industries, many women feel it's necessary to dress a bit sexier or to be a bit provocative in their photos to capture their audience's attention. To each her own, but you may be sending out a message that is *less than* professional.

This happens with some men, too. I recall once seeing a man with a bath-robe in front of a fire in his profile photo, and another of a man with his shirt unbuttoned so his chest hair was peeking out; still, others seemed to have a "come hither" seductive pose in their photo.

If it's not a pose you would use for the most important interview of your life or to show to your most important client, it's probably not a pose you should be using on LinkedIn.

By the way, if you've sized your photo appropriately and zoomed it in, your cleavage (or chest hair) shouldn't even be an issue. We should only see a small glimpse of your neckline and anything that shouldn't be seen should be out of frame.

Size it right.

Your face should be 50-60% of the size of the LinkedIn headshot photo circle. Consider that about half (or more!) of your connections will be looking at your LinkedIn profile on a mobile phone.

If your photo shows you from your head to waist, visitors can barely see your face when viewing your profile on their phone. Plus, the further back your face, the less important you seem, the less impressive you seem, and the more diminutive you seem.

A zoomed in photo (face at 50-60% of the circle frame) makes you seem more important, more approachable, and more personable. It's a subtle change that can make a *huge* difference.

When I am uploading my photo, I try to zoom it in so that my face (from the top of my forehead to my chin) fills in the top middle box and center box of LinkedIn's nine-box frame.

Set your photo visibility to PUBLIC so everyone can see you.

Some people will not accept invitations from people who do not have a photo on their account. In fact, I've read that having a photo set to public will increase your profile views by as much as 21%[8].

You may not even be aware of your photo settings, so I recommend you stop and check them right now.[9] I was once at a board meeting when a fellow board member saw this setting and her photo was set to show *only to her connections*. She wasn't even aware of this limitation, and it was not intentional.

Use a CURRENT photo.

I recommend you obtain a new headshot every 2-5 years. Don't be "that guy" or "that woman" whose photo was clearly taken before LinkedIn launched. We all age. It's better to represent the real you, circa now.

I've been at networking events where I meet a person for the first time and discover that they are at least 20 years older than their LinkedIn photo depicts. It's always a bit jarring. Plus, I feel I've been misled a bit on who the person really is. When your photo is outdated, I start to wonder what else you might be hiding. By comparison, a current photo sends a message of trust and transparency.

---

8   blog.linkedin.com/2017/march/14/linkedin-profile-photo-tips-introducing -photo-filters-and-editing
9   Read these instructions to check your settings: www.linkedin.com/help/linked in/answer/31?hiptopic=feed

Any opportunity you have to get a new headshot photo, get one! If some-one ever says, "oh, I almost didn't know it was you!" when meeting you (after you've connected on LinkedIn), it might be time for a new photo.

> Your LinkedIn headshot is the equivalent of being able to SEE the pie at a bakery before making the purchase. Appearance *matters*, and just like a pie wants to be at its personal best in the bakery case, you should strive to make sure your headshot photo shows YOU at your personal best, too.

My favorite pie is raspberry, YUM!
~ Issa Forrest
www.linkedin.com/in/issaforrest

Chapter 19:

Optimizing Your ABOUT Statement

"Most economic fallacies derive from the tendency to assume that there is a fixed pie, that one party can gain only at the expense of another."
~ *Milton Friedman*

Your "About" statement is one of the most important areas on your LinkedIn profile, as it provides a space for you to tell us your story. When reviewing client profiles, these are several common MISTAKES I see:

MISTAKE 1: The About statement is identical to the professional summary you have at the top of your resume. Why is this incorrect? The goal of your resume is to help you find a new job. The goal of your ABOUT statement is to share your professional story with visitors throughout your career as it evolves. You may use your LinkedIn periodically throughout your career for job search, but it's not an ongoing search.

MISTAKE 2: The About statement is written in the third person. "Brenda is an experienced marketing leader…" Your LinkedIn profile should read as though YOU are speaking to me, and therefore your About statement should be written in the first person; "I am an experienced marketing leader…" By changing it from third person to first person, you are able to make an immediate connection with your profile visitors. Pretend I'm sitting right across the table from you and I'm your IDEAL TARGET AUDIENCE. How do you describe yourself? Not in the third person, I hope!

MISTAKE 3: Not making maximum use of the viewable area before people have to click "see more." Keep in mind that most people will NOT click "see more," so what you have in the first three lines is all they see. The RIGHT people will click "see more," but only if you've given them a compelling reason to do so.

MISTAKE 4: Not maximizing the total or viewable character limit. Quite often, I'll see an About statement written with about eight lines of copy in one long boring paragraph (sorry, but it *is* long and boring and I'm not going to read it and neither will most people). Or, the person has two sentences and an extra line break in-between the sentences which pushes the second sentence out of the viewable area.

MISTAKE 5: The About statement is written so broadly that it's not clear to me who the person is looking to connect with on LinkedIn or *why*. It might be too short, rambling, or inconsistent with what I know about the person.

MISTAKE 6: There's no About statement at all. Of all the mistakes, this is probably the biggest one of all. Something is ALWAYS better than nothing.

Perhaps you identify with one of the mistakes outlined above; maybe you're not even aware it's a mistake. You're not alone, and I'm here to explain and guide you through the process of creating an AMAZING About statement. A properly written About statement will help to increase your profile views, keep people on your profile longer, and help you to reach your business goals. So, let's get started.

I'm going to walk you through optimizing your About statement by splitting this into two areas: technical aspects and content suggestions.

TECHNICAL ASPECTS:

➤ Although you can include up to 2,600 characters in your About statement, only three lines appear before the viewer has to click to "see more."

➤ About 30-45 words (290 characters) show on desktop view, but even fewer (10-12 words) display on mobile view. Therefore, you need to make the first few words compelling in order to prompt a viewer of your profile to click "see more." Look at your About statement right now in desktop view and then on the mobile app to see for yourself. I recommend that when writing your About statement, you focus on making it front-loaded with the most important sentence FIRST. Your goal is to get them to stay on your profile and click "see more." Look at your About statement right now. *Is it interesting? Compelling? Written to attract your ideal target audience?* If not, you've got some work to do.

➤ Your About statement does not allow for HTML formatting. This means there is not a menu in LinkedIn to add bullets, bolding, underlining, italics, or hyperlinks. All of these items can make copy easier to read; without them, it can make for a very text-heavy and BORING section. Therefore, I recommend you consider using several of the following items to make your About statement easier to read:

> **ALL CAPS for section headings**. Just like I've done through-out this book, using all caps signals IMPORTANT words to the readers and sets up a new section of your profile. BUT PLEASE DO NOT WRITE YOUR ENTIRE ABOUT STATEMENT IN ALL CAPS BECAUSE IT WILL LOOK LIKE YOU ARE YELLING. All caps used sparingly, though, can create emphasis and improve readability.

> **Paragraph breaks.** But, wait, you're thinking... didn't I just tell you *not* to use paragraph breaks in the first three lines?

Yes. But after that, I recommend adding in paragraph breaks at about every third line. Keep in mind that three lines on desktop equals about six lines on mobile. You want to make it easy for your profile viewer to quickly skim through your profile. Paragraph breaks create white space, making your profile easier to read. In marketing speak, we like to call this method creating, "short, snackable chunks of copy."

> **The use of symbols such as ">" as bullets.** This works fine if you're writing or editing your About statement right in LinkedIn and you are looking for a quick fix. This is probably a good time to issue a warning: DO NOT WRITE YOUR ABOUT STATEMENT IN LINKEDIN. IF YOU DO SO, LINKEDIN WILL HICCUP IN THE MIDDLE OF THIS AND YOU WILL LOSE ALL OF YOUR WORK. NO, IT DOES NOT SAVE. YES, IT'S GONE. YES, YOU WILL NEED TO TYPE IT ALL OVER AGAIN.

Sorry for the all caps there. I know that was hard to read but it's even harder to rewrite the masterpiece that is your About statement when you lose all of your work. Instead, I recommend you use Word or some similar program to create and save your About statement as you go. Then, copy and paste it into LinkedIn.

> **The use of emojis as bullets.** My trick for this is to create your About statement in a Word document with bullets for any bulleted lists, then paste the text into LinkedIn in the desktop version. Then, save it and open up your profile on the LinkedIn app. Go into your About statement and access your emoji keyboard. Keep in mind here that you should keep your emojis related to your business and career. Also, don't use too many different emojis because it will start to make your LinkedIn profile look like a junky internet site from 2000. Ick.

CONTENT SUGGESTIONS

Okay, now that we've covered the technical aspects, let's talk about the words you use. Overall, your About statement should be a professional yet conversational description of YOU written in your own words and to your IDEAL TARGET AUDIENCE. You are not writing your About statement for the world. It's fine if the world sees it, but your goal is to reach your target audience and you'll have better luck doing so if you write your About statement as if you're speaking *directly* to that audience.

First, consider a compelling introduction in your very first sentence. I like to think of that first sentence as an extension or continuation of your headline.

Some people like to start with their elevator pitch: a 30-second description of yourself that you'd share if you were in an elevator with your ideal target audience.

Overall, your summary should tell us your story. Think about how you describe yourself to others or how others describe you. This section should be a summary of who you are as a professional– not just a summary of your current role.

Your About statement should be written in the first person (I, my, me, etc.). As mentioned earlier, this makes it feel as though you are talking *directly* to the person reading your profile.

Still struggling with how to tell us your story? Here are a few suggestions.

Review those on LinkedIn who share your job title to see what they have in *their* About statements. Reading these may help to inspire you. Plus, you're getting the benefit of seeing what your target audience sees.

Do you have any recommendations? If so, review those to see what common themes people say about you and include those in your About statement.

> **Consider one of these lines to begin your About statement.**
> Feel free to modify it to fit your own voice and experiences:
>
> ➤ I chose to be a [job title] in [industry] due to my love of [skill] and my desire to [achievement].
> ➤ I discovered my love for [industry] during [description]. Helping organizations [goal] is [adjective].
> ➤ The most rewarding part of being involved with [job category] is...
> ➤ In my role as [job title], I help [audience] with [service you provide/problem you solve].
> ➤ I became a [job title] after a XX year career in [industry] due to my desire to [your company mission].

Include a few personal / career goals or inspirational quotes to help give your About statement some personalization. These have been powerful for me in that they help to pull back my professional exterior to reveal who I am as a person.

Include a list of your top 8-10 areas of expertise in a running keyword list with the heading 'SPECIALTIES' toward the end of your About statement. I have this in my profile and I periodically review and update my list based on my business focus. I include this, not necessarily for you as a human being to read (although I don't mind that you read it), but more for the fact that it helps my profile to come up in more searches on LinkedIn.

The technique here is similar to that of SEO, or search engine optimization. If I want to come up in more searches for LinkedIn strategy, LinkedIn team training, public speaking, or conference presenter, then I have to make sure that those keywords appear in multiple places and multiple times throughout my profile. The more often those words appear, the more likely my profile will come up in search results on LinkedIn.

Think about LinkedIn the same way you think about Google: it's a giant search engine. If you want to come up to the top of search results, you need an optimized profile that is keyword rich.

I have heard some say that the algorithm is catching up with this technique, but I've not seen a noticeable dip in my profile views or search results, so I will continue to keep this keyword list in my profile for now. LinkedIn is always changing, so this will be an area I keep my eye on for the future.

On that note, keep in mind that LinkedIn likes to see fresh, active profiles. Therefore, I will review my profile at least once a quarter to make keyword and phrase changes. Not only is this helping to make sure my profile is evolving as my business grows, but it's also helping to keep me at the top of search results and drive more profile views.

Please look at my About statement now as reference. Look at it in both desktop and mobile views. If you like any of the techniques I use, feel free to replicate them on your own profile. Don't copy and paste (that would be plagiarism), but please do let my profile inspire you!

Visit and view my profile as often as you'd like. I always tell people that this is what I do for a living; my goal is to incorporate techniques to help bring me up in more searches and keep people on my profile longer. I am flattered when I see readers and clients looking at my profile because I know they are doing their homework!

Here are common elements I use when rewriting ABOUT statements for my clients:
First, start with an intriguing introduction that immediately connects you with your target audience.

If you're using LinkedIn for business development, end this first section with a call-to-action and contact info (either a website, email, and/or phone number). If you're using LinkedIn as a job seeker in career transition, start with a compelling statement that illustrates your personal brand and how you're different than other people who share your job title, and end this section with your email address.

In any case, end the first paragraph with contact info and maximize the text before "see more."

Then, a paragraph break (after the "see more" break).

Then, describe more about your current professional role, including a broad overview of your company's products or services. If you're in career transition, tell us a bit more about what skills and experiences you'll bring to your next employer and how it will help that employer meet their business goals.

After this, include details summarizing your career to-date, connecting the dots to where you are today.

I recommend ending with a few personal statements. These might include goals, leadership quotes, or other items that pack a nice punch at the end and keep people reading along. I recommend pulling back the professional exterior to show your profile visitors that there's a real person here.

Then, review to make sure you're at 2,600 characters or fewer. That's it!

Still struggling? **Look at my profile for some inspiration.** And just start *somewhere*. You can always come back later and edit your About statement as you continue to work on your LinkedIn profile.

My favorite pie is pecan.
~ Jan McIntyre
www.linkedin.com/in/jan-mcintyre-mi

Chapter 20:

Experience

"So the pie isn't perfect? Cut it into wedges.
Stay in control, and never panic."
~ Martha Stewart

The Experience section of your profile is one of those areas you may not give much thought or attention to, but it can really be a huge asset in helping you reach your goals on LinkedIn. The way I look at it is this: if someone is taking the time to read through your profile, why not give them something interesting to read?

The biggest two mistakes I see people making in their Experience section are:

1. **Not linking to your LinkedIn company page. It's not linked if your logo is a gray building avatar.** I like to say, "Gray is *not* OK" to help you remember this. If it's a gray building avatar, that means you either do not have a LinkedIn company page OR your page is not properly linked to your profile. If it's the latter, you can fix this by editing the company name. Just delete it and re-add it until the logo appears.

   If it's the former, it's a gray avatar because your company does not have a company page on LinkedIn, or because you have not properly linked it to your company page. If that's the case, this is a missed opportunity. Even if you work for yourself, you should have a company page on LinkedIn. When you set up a company page, you have the opportunity to add in your company logo to the page, which makes that boring gray building avatar go away.

No company logo? People will question if you really did work there. Or, if you're self-employed, they will question whether your company REALLY exists or if you're just working out of your basement. Even if you ARE working out of your basement, that company logo means something. It helps to legitimize you in the eyes of your profile viewers.

If you're unemployed and in career transition, read my blog with tips on what to put there and why.[10]

2. **Not including any text or description to accompany this section.** This is an opportunity to be a gracious host and to help show people around your profile. If I don't see a description, this is an immediate opportunity for improvement.

Are you ready to optimize your Experience section? Great! Let's get started. First, make sure your job title is accurate, spelled correctly (you wouldn't believe how many "marketing *mangers*" there are on LinkedIn right now: 1.95M according to my search results!), and take a look at your dates.

I recommend that, if you're a senior leader, you consider omitting the month you started at your position for anything beyond your current role. Less detail is better, in my opinion… unless keeping the month on there makes it appear you stayed *longer* at the role.

Next, let's move into the description section (you'll see this when you click the pencil icon).

---

10   www.linkedin.com/pulse/career-transition-employer-options-brenda-meller

You may notice "Employment type" as a new drop-down in this area. Personally, I haven't done anything to any of my Experience sections with this feature on LinkedIn. I could see how it could help if you're an intern, but I don't see how this would otherwise benefit me. Nor have I seen any other LinkedIn experts highlighting how this can help you come up in more search results, or how it helps those in career transition.

My personal feeling is this feature helps recruiters and LinkedIn as a whole, but I don't see how it benefits us as members. Feel free to fill this in if you're so inclined; I don't see how it could *hurt* your efforts!

For location, you can either choose the metro area or leave this blank. The way I see it, your location is already indicated in your top header card. I've added my cities in.

Be sure NOT to check "Update my industry" or "Update my headline" here. I prefer to make these changes manually in the top header card, and by clicking "Update my headline," your carefully crafted headline disappears and is replaced with "job title at company" for this position.

Next, look for the box titled, "Description." This is where the magic of your Experience section occurs. In this box, you have the opportunity to tell your story for each experience in 2,000 characters or less.

I recommend that you begin with a one- to three-sentence description of your company. Why? Because someone looking at your profile may not be familiar with your company. Adding the description helps them to place you and your company. If your company has a company page on LinkedIn, a really easy way to obtain this description is to click your employer logo, then visit the "About" section of their LinkedIn company page. There should be a few sentences that you can copy and paste into your experience section.

See? I like to make things easy for you. I'm lazy when it comes to marketing, and I'll always search to see what's already been done. And I also like to see brand consistency in your messaging and what your employer uses.

Then, if you're still working there, list the service or product offerings of the company. By doing so, you are demonstrating that you are a highly engaged, brand ambassador for your company. You are showing your employer that you support your own products and services. You are helping your target audience learn more about the products and services you offer. I recommend you put these in a bulleted list. You should be writing this whole section in an external place like Word where you're copying/pasting, so be sure to use the bulleted list feature there.

Just like as in your About section, LinkedIn does NOT save as you're working in this section, and YOU WILL LOSE YOUR WORK if you don't save this as you go in an external document. Yes, this has happened to me. Ugh!

If you're in a sales role, at the end of this paragraph, include your email and/or phone number for those interested in learning more.

MAKE IT EASY FOR PEOPLE WHO WANT TO DO BUSINESS WITH YOU!

Yes, all caps was necessary. People don't want to dig around to find your contact info. Even if your email isn't clickable, it makes it easy for people to get a hold of you.

If you're not in a sales role and you're still working at this company, at the end of this paragraph, include a web page, email, and/or phone number for your sales department for people who may be interested in doing business with you.

If you're no longer working for the company skip the second paragraph and move to my recommendations for your role (next paragraph).

Then, in the third paragraph, provide a quick summary of what you do in this role, including a few key achievements (if applicable). It's OK to copy and paste a bit from your resume, but I would not recommend this to be exactly the same as your resume. Your LinkedIn profile should give viewers a flavor of what you have to offer, but it should not read exactly the same as your resume.

Think about these achievements from the perspective of your IDEAL target audience. Would they care that you were named top salesperson of the year? Or that you reduced expenses by 25% for your company? If not, skip it on your LinkedIn Experience section, and show them in your resume instead.

> Remember: the goal of your resume is to find a job.
> The goal of your LinkedIn is to help you connect with your ideal target audience. If you're not a job seeker in career transition, your LinkedIn profile should NOT look like a resume.

This is especially important if you are looking for a new job and you don't want your current employer to know. It's a red flag for me that someone is looking when their current experience description paragraph reads exactly like their resume. Even if the person is in-between successes and actively in career transition, I'd prefer to scale back the description and follow the same formula– excluding the contact info to do business with the company. If they aren't paying you a paycheck, you don't need to send them any business.

End with your specialties in a paragraph list. Remember, it is OK to repeat specialties (skills) you've included in your About statement, and repeat these again in your SKILLS section. The more often a keyword appears on your profile, the more likely your name will appear in search results for that word/phrase.

FAQs

Experience

Q: What if my employer no longer exists and there is a gray avatar?
A: Skip it. In this case, gray is OK. This is becoming more common as time goes on. Some companies didn't exist when LinkedIn was created, or have since gone out of business and no longer have a company page.

Q: Should I list all of my previous jobs?
A: It depends. I recommend you include positions only if it helps to tell your story and include details if relevant to your current and future career goals.

Remember: You are sculpting your LinkedIn profile for your IDEAL TARGET AUDIENCE. If you worked in retail to put yourself through college and that sales clerk job is no longer relevant now that you have professional experience, delete it.

When you're filling out a job application, make sure you are being honest with the employer. If they ask for every job since college, tell them. But, on LinkedIn, you can omit details and/or employers who don't help to tell the unique story of who you are today and who you wish to become in the future.

Q: What should I do if I have a gap? I stayed home to take care of my ailing parent / raise my kids.
A: First of all, congratulations to you for having your priorities straight. You are an amazing human being and I commend you for shifting to family when they needed you.

You can leave the gap and explain it in your cover letter, or you can fill it in creatively with something that describes the time gap. I once saw someone's profile which read:

Experience: CEO of [Last Name] Household

Year – Year

I had the honor and privilege of raising human beings during the first few years of their lives. I served as CFO, nutritionist, activities director, training & development, and coach/mentor.

This approach is not for everyone, but it does help to explain in "corporate speak" any gaps you wish to explain.

Q: *I was laid off from my last employer. How soon do I need to put in an end date? I haven't found a job yet.*
A: Personally, I wouldn't rush to change the end date because it could impact your ability to come up in search results. If you keep the employer on there though, make sure that you do disable anniversary notifications, unless you want to be congratulated by your network on your work anniversary date (ouch).

I have heard that not having a current employer negatively affects your search results, so if it's within the first six months to a year of leaving the employer, you could omit an end date. You definitely need to be up-front when applying for positions that you are no longer employed and, if asked why your LinkedIn does not show that you left, you could say you didn't get around to it yet OR that you heard about the algorithm penalizing people who do not have a current employer.

To be honest, I don't think many hiring managers or recruiters will notice, and if they do, they will probably conclude you haven't updated your LinkedIn yet– especially if your resume shows an end date.

Another option: If you are giving advice to people in your network OR being paid for consulting work while looking for a new position: POOF! You are a consultant. Add a new employer to your LinkedIn profile and create a company page.

I created Meller Marketing years ago when I was dabbling with my side hustle. When I was in career transition, I moved it to the top section in my Experience and added this note in the description (feel free to copy/paste):

> While I am looking for that one LinkedIn connection to lead me to my next dream job, I am staying active in the marketing community with project work and consulting projects at Meller Marketing.

This essentially tells recruiters, "I'm open to a full-time opportunity. I'm seeking a full-time opportunity. But I'm not sitting around on the couch waiting for it. I'm keeping busy by answering the call of people in my network who value my expertise and who are willing to pay me to help them while I'm in transition."

On this note, make sure that your TOP Experience is your current employer who is supplying your paycheck. I do include board positions as well as side hustles in my Experience section, but I want it to be clear that the TOP Experience is my primary role. Important to note here too that the top Experience is the one that shows in your *top* header card.

Q: I serve on a board. Could this go in my Experience section?
A: Yes! I recommend adding your board affiliation to your LinkedIn profile, just below your current employer. Or, if you're in career transition, put it as your Top company in your experience section. By doing so, you are giving visibility to organizations where you serve.

Hover over any of the Experience sections and to the right side, you'll see the stack of four lines (referred to as the "hamburger" symbol because it looks like a stacked hamburger) and you can drag and drop to re-order your Experiences.

You may wish to include MEDIA in each Experience section as well. I recommend uploading media for your current employer and perhaps previous employers, if it helps to shape your brand story.

Q: Does adding media help you to come up in more searches on LinkedIn?
A: I've not heard any data to show that including media on your profile helps you to come up in more searches. However, I recommend including media to help supplement any text you have added to your profile. Media is visually interesting and may prompt profile visitors to stay on your page longer, helping you to achieve your business or career goals.

And, as always, feel free to look at my profile for inspiration on how I set up my Experience for each employer.

I love blueberry pie. Apple, too! :)
~ Albert Freedman
www.linkedin.com/in/albert-freedman-29505876

Chapter 21:

Skills

"Instead, I have an abundance mentality:
When people are genuinely happy
at the successes of others, the pie gets larger."
~ *Stephen Covey*

Skills & Endorsements is one of the most overlooked areas of your LinkedIn profile, and one where you can make a few quick changes in just a few minutes.

Here's what I recommend:

First, click on the pencil icon and go through and review your current skills. Delete any that aren't relevant to your career or your future career path. Remember: the goal here is to keep skills that are RELEVANT and remove skills that are irrelevant.

Next, look at the three skills that are pinned to the top. The first time you look at these skills, the pins will be set to the top three skills based on number of endorsements. However, they may not be the top three skills you want to be known for.

Keep in mind here that most people will NOT click "See more" to look at your other skills. They will only look at the top three and they will immediately make a judgement call on what they see.

Look at your top three skills. Are these the top three you want to be known for? If not, you CAN and SHOULD pin other skills in those places.

The top three currently listed are those skills which you have received the most endorsements for to-date, but you can make changes to the order and to which skills are pinned here. After you move the pins, they stay in place. LinkedIn will not reorder the top three again.

The top three should be those that are most relevant to your career expertise, to your business goals, and to your ideal target audience. When you're satisfied with the list and your three top pins, save to exit.

You can have up to 50 skills on your profile, and I recommend you use all 50 places to specify your top skills. Having 50 skills increases the chances of you appearing in search results. Plus, it helps to tell the story of your expertise to people who visit this section.

NOTE: If you're well-established in your career, I recommend you OMIT any skills that are lower-level or entry-level skills. These might include skills such as Excel, Word, PowerPoint, Time Management, or other similar-sounding skills.

When you click on the "Add a new skill" link (next to the pencil icon), you'll see a few suggestions from LinkedIn based on your profile data. Click the plus button (+) to add any that are relevant, then perhaps add in any other skills missing from your profile.

Still not at 50 skills? Do what I do. Look at other LinkedIn members who share your job title: *what skills do they include on their profiles?* Chances are, you have those areas of expertise, too, and you can therefore add those same skills to YOUR profile.

My friend Shawna Ramsey (www.linkedin.com/in/shawna01) asked if there is a master list of all skills anywhere on LinkedIn.

> Not at the time of publication, unfortunately. I found one site[11] that mentioned there are 35,000 skills in the LinkedIn "skills" list. However, I've also found that you can create a CUSTOM skill, which leaves the skills list only to your imagination!

Remember, it is OK to repeat skills that you have included in your About statement, and repeat these again in your SKILLS section. The more often a keyword appears on your profile, the more likely your profile will appear in search results for that word/phrase.

Finally, let's talk about Endorsements of your skills. Yes, having endorsements for your top skills does help with bringing you up in more search results on LinkedIn, but I don't worry about endorsements on my own profile too much.

Instead, I recommend you do this: when you are viewing someone's profile, take a moment to give them a few endorsements for skills you know they have. By doing so, you are creating social media karma and you're helping to make them smile.

Who knows? They may even repay the favor and endorse YOU for some of your skills, too!

I have heard that having 99+ endorsements for a skill helps you to come up in more searches for that skill. And knowing that "people are lazy" (no, I don't really think this... but it WILL help you remember this tip) and that most won't click "see more" to see your *full* list of skills, I will sometimes reorder my skills list to move skills that have 99+ endorsements to push them lower in the list, and move other skills into the top three positions so they collect more endorsements.

Also, keep in mind that you can get creative here and *invent* your own skills. In fact, I have added "Getting People Out of LinkedIn Jail" as one

---

11   www.omnicoreagency.com/linkedin-statistics/

of my top three skills on my profile. No, "LinkedIn Jail" is not a physical place. But if you've ever had your account locked due to violating a rule or their terms of service, you know what this place is. And having this at the top of my skills list helps me to differentiate from other consultants who also specialize in LinkedIn Strategy.

Another way to add new skills is to review skills you have been endorsed for from your network that aren't on your profile yet. Use caution here. I was once endorsed for "accounting" by a network connection; I wouldn't consider myself an accounting expert by any stretch of the imagination. I DO know that pie is also sometimes called "pi" and celebrated on 3.14 (March 14) but I think that would be geometry and not accounting, right?

My favorite pie is pumpkin.
~ Lauren (Rossi) Lawrence
www.linkedin.com/in/lnrossilawrence

Chapter 22:

Giving and Requesting LinkedIn Recommendations

"Well, she didn't ask for anything! She was nice as pie."
~ Laura Ingalls,
defending Nellie Olson to her sister Mary Ingalls
on Little House on the Prairie, Season 2, Episode 12

Want to grow your business? Ask your clients for *their* help.

Remember the "trade show table" effect. I've talked about this before but it's worth repeating. It's been proven time and time again that **people like social proof.** They like to see that other people are interested in your product or service. If it's worth waiting in line for, it *has* to be valuable.

Same goes with your business. If you have a number of testimonials from satisfied clients, your future clients may be more apt to sign on with you.

These testimonials can be even more valuable because now they are linked to our professional social media accounts, so there is a high degree of credibility.

The fact is that people believe more in what OTHERS say about your business than in what YOU say about your business. After all, you're selling. Other people are *telling*.

Do you have a client who LOVES your business? Ask him or her for a testimonial in the form of a LinkedIn recommendation on your LinkedIn profile. While you're at it, you may want to ask this person for permission to use their logos in your client list in your marketing materials, too.

Feel free to borrow my email technique for this request and modify the language to fit your voice.

Subject: A favor to help me grow Meller Marketing

As I'm growing Meller Marketing, it's beneficial to demonstrate my experience by telling people which clients I've helped and by including testimonials on my website and in my proposals.

1. *Could I showcase your [client name] logo on my website (www. mellermarketing.com)? I'd be happy to link your logo to your web page [insert their web page address here].*

2. *Would you be willing to offer me a recommendation on LinkedIn? If you could speak to my LinkedIn expertise and the helpfulness of the insights I offered, that would be great. If you agree, I'll send the LinkedIn recommendation request to you to help make it easy for you to do so.*

Thanks for consideration of this request.

Sincerely,
Brenda Meller
brenda@mellermarketing.com

Feel free to use the above to send to your TOP customers only. I wouldn't send this unless you're pretty confident they will be OK with your request. After all, you want RAVING fans to give you ENTHUSIASTIC reviews.

Create social media karma: GIVE recommendations

Have you ever given someone in your network a LinkedIn recommendation? *You should*.

By giving someone a recommendation, you are paying it forward. And by "it" I mean you're creating positive karma.

The real power of LinkedIn is in our connections. Giving a well-deserved recommendation helps you to strengthen those connections.

When you choose references on a job application, you're going to choose the three people who will give you a glowing reference. But remember, employers know that too.

Plus, we don't always know what your relationship is with that particular reference and just how credible they are. The reference could be a brother-in-law, classmate, or neighbor.

LinkedIn recommendations are tied to a profile and that means it's *their* professional credibility on the line. I know that if I'm asked, I will think twice before giving a LinkedIn recommendation. If I don't really stand behind the person or know the person well on a professional level, I will not give them a recommendation. And I choose my words wisely if I am giving a recommendation.

All of that said, there are a LOT of great people in my network to whom I have given recommendations. Who comes to mind for you? Think of rockstar team players. Phenomenal clients. Managers who could write books about inspirational leadership. Interns who have worked their tails off.

Here are a few selected recommendations I've given. I hope these inspire you to write someone a recommendation today. Also, while you're at it, check out their LinkedIn profiles and consider inviting these individuals to connect to you. Tell them that Brenda sent you. It will make their day.

Dr. Rita Fields (www.linkedin.com/in/drritafields)

"An amazing keynote presenter. Every time I have the chance to hear Rita speak, I discover new things about myself. She has helped me strengthen my beliefs and confidence in who I am and who I wish to be. Rita is a powerful presenter who engages her entire audience. She draws from her professional experience and education to tell stories that are poignant and memorable, yet relatable. You will laugh and you will nod in agreement with her observations and philosophies. If you have the chance to hire Rita for a speaking event, do it. She is amazing."

Patti Harrison (www.linkedin.com/in/patti-harrison-20a9507)

"I began working with Patti and her team in 2008 and always had an exceptional experience working with Patti and team. Harrison Media provided all management and placement of paid media for Walsh for almost a decade. I would (and have) recommend Patti and Harrison Media to any marketer seeking to outsource their advertising placement. Assigning advertising management to an outside expert like Patti frees you up so you can focus on oversight of all areas of your marketing leadership. (full recommendation on my profile)

Sherry Kenyon, MA, SPHR (www.linkedin.com/in/sherrykenyon)

"I had the pleasure of working with Sherry while at Pitney Bowes. From the very first presentation to our group, Sherry was a true professional who worked to help realize the corporate vision at the business unit level. Sherry is focused on employee engagement at all levels within the organization,

while ensuring that all parties are in compliance with corporate guidelines. I am proud to have had the pleasure of working with Sherry. She is an asset to the organization."

Hiba Sultan Hariri (www.linkedin.com/in/hibasultanh)
"Hiba is an extremely talented graphic designer. I would highly recommend her for any position in graphic design. She has an impressive portfolio and a great eye for design. In addition to continually producing an impressive list of projects, often proposing multiple concept ideas. Hiba is open to feedback to ensure her clients (internal or external) are satisfied. However, she is also able to professionally and tactfully push back when a requested change would violate brand standards. I enjoyed working with Hiba at Walsh and welcome the opportunity provide referrals for any positions where she applies in the future."

Strive for balance... in THEIR favor.
Have you ever viewed someone's LinkedIn profile who has been given 20 LinkedIn recommendations but has never given someone else a recommendation? Think about the message that sends.

It becomes obvious that that person is a TAKER and not a giver.

It is obvious that they are using LinkedIn selfishly for their own gain, with no thought to others in their network.

Is that the kind of person you want to do business with? To hire to join your team? Or to refer business to?

Probably not.

Here's what I recommend: Strive to always have more recommendations GIVEN than received on your profile. This sends a subtle message that you value your connections; it also forces you to continually think of one or two more people you could recommend.

Struggling with *who* to recommend? Be strategic and consider the following points:

> Current or former team members or coworkers.
> Current or former managers or company leaders who've inspired you.
> Fellow members of professional groups you are active in.
> Members of your community groups, religious communities, or volunteer groups.
> Vendors, consultants, or employees of agencies you have hired to help you on a project or ongoing basis.
> Leaders of chambers or organizations you belong to.
> People you have seen speak at events: keynotes, workshops, or even emcees.
> If you've been laid off or downsized, consider others who were laid off at the same time as you. It's OK to exchange recommendations (you give them one and they give you one) but try not to do this with *every* recommendation.

You do have to be connected to them on LinkedIn, and they do have to accept your recommendation in order for it to show on their profile. For this reason, I like to send them a "heads up" message via LinkedIn or an email that the recommendation is on its way and to look for it.

When I review your recommendation section, I look for two items:

1. **At least one recommendation given and received in the current year**. I can tell immediately if you've only used LinkedIn in the past when in job search mode, and I can also tell the last time you started thinking about a career change based on the dates of your recommendations.

You may have a flurry of invitations given to you right before you made a move. However, if you're always adding in a recommendation (or two or three) each year, I can't tell when or if you may be considering a move.

2. **More recommendations given than received**. This shows that you are focused on others. It's common to see 2-3 recommendations given but none received. I was recently in a coaching session with a business development executive and he realized he had a pending recommendation on his profile from six months ago. At the time of our session, he had no recommendations given OR received. Eek.

The great thing about LinkedIn recommendations is that you are given the chance to review them before deciding if you'd like to add them to your profile. Typos? Request an edit before you accept it. Incorrect information or a recommendation from someone you'd prefer not to align yourself with? You can gently message them back or just ignore the invite. I've done this and it is appropriate to do so. Or, you can accept the recommendation but hide it from your profile. If you do so, the recommendation will not appear on their profile, either.

How to give someone a LinkedIn recommendation
Hopefully I've convinced you to give a few recommendations. The process is pretty easy:

1. Be on the person's profile.

2. Look for the "MORE" button and click it. One option will be "recommend." Click on it.

3. Follow the instructions from LinkedIn.[12]

---

12   Here are the instructions from LinkedIn: www.linkedin.com/help/linkedin/answer/97/recommending-someone-on-linkedin?lang=en

4. When you include the recommendation text, make sure you give it some substantial context. Don't just say, "Chris is a great person. I would recommend him!" Instead, say, "Chris is a great ambassador for his organization. He is passionate and empowered when speaking in front of groups, whether the audience includes high school students or senior leaders of the community. I highly recommend Chris as an inspirational speaker."

How to request a LinkedIn recommendation
This part may feel awkward for some of you, but I want to remind you that you bought this book and you're still reading it because you know I have nuggets of wisdom.

I remember in daycare, my kids' teachers would use a technique called a "no thank you bite" to get the kids to try new foods at lunchtime.

The concept was this: even if the child did not want what was offered, they had to try at least one little bite. Then, if they still didn't want it, they would say, "no thank you, I don't like that."

It's a powerful technique for us grown-ups, too.

I want you to TRY this. Request a LinkedIn recommendation, even if it feels awkward. Start by making a list of 3-5 people in your professional network on LinkedIn who love working with you.

Maybe it's a client who's been with you for ten years and always sends you referrals.

Maybe it's the boss who tries to hire you away every time they change jobs.

Maybe it's the president of your local community group who raves about how much of an asset you are to their organization.

There are probably a few people in your network who you know would be HAPPY to give you a LinkedIn recommendation. Think of those people who have said, "Brenda, if there's ever anything you need, let me know."

If you're not sure if they will give you a recommendation, they're probably not the right person to ask.

Here are some magic keywords or conversations that could lead to a recommendation:

➤ Wow! You are amazing. Thanks so much for helping me (or my business)!
➤ I have really enjoyed working with you on this project. I learned so much from you.
➤ You are an outstanding leader. You have inspired me and so many of us.
➤ You are the best hire I've ever made.
➤ I was referred to you by [Client A]. HINT: you should ask Client A for a LinkedIn recommendation.
➤ Just a quick email to let you know how much I appreciate working with you. (These typically include a specific compliment of your work on a recent project or handling a difficult situation. Personally, I print these and put these in a "Rainy Day File" that I pull out and read when I'm having a bad day.)
➤ I have enjoyed serving on the board / committee with you.

My favorite pie is strawberry rhubarb :)
~ Mike Podesta
www.linkedin.com/in/mike-podesta-44645ba3

Chapter 23:

Your Contact Info

Annie, my sweet, have you got those pies?
~ Harry Bailey in "It's a Wonderful Life"

If you are using LinkedIn for business development or to build up your personal brand, your Contact Info section is one area that will greatly benefit from some small but powerful changes.

Click on "Contact Info" now and let's review each section.

Your profile
Underneath this heading, your profile viewers will see your LinkedIn URL. If it hasn't been simplified, your URL will have a bunch of random numbers and letters at the end of your URL. You can click this URL to go to the Public Profile Settings page to make the update. Refer to Chapter 10 for instructions on how to simplify your LinkedIn URL.

Websites
LinkedIn allows users to feature up to three websites in your contact info section. One of the BIGGEST mistakes I see on LinkedIn profiles? Websites not added or listed incorrectly in "see contact info."

If people want to do business with you, MAKE IT EASY FOR THEM. Don't neglect this section. Every so often, I'll visit a client's profile and point out that the website listed is actually that of their former employer.

Keep in mind that the "websites" you list don't all need to be your company website homepage. You can pick secondary pages that list your key products, services, events, or offers. Or you can showcase top-performing blogs, send people to your e-newsletter sign-up form, or point them to your speaker sizzle real.

You may wish to consider including professional organization websites of which you are a member. This is a great technique for those in a career transition who want to demonstrate that they are keeping active in their professional community.

You can also showcase organizations whose board you serve on.

An important consideration… what are the top three web pages (outside of LinkedIn) that you would want your IDEAL TARGET AUDIENCE to visit after looking at your profile?

Regardless of which links you add, and even if you do list your company website, change the website type from "COMPANY" to "OTHER" and add a few words (up to 30 characters) to describe the link.

Again, MAKE IT EASY FOR YOUR AUDIENCE. If I were to list www.meller-marketing.com and designate it as "Company Website" from the LinkedIn dropdown, it would show as: www.mellermarketing.com (Company website)

But if instead I choose "Other" from the drop-down and type in some keywords, it would show as:

www.mellermarketing.com (LinkedIn Strategy Services)

You have 30 characters to describe where you want them to go. Choose words that are descriptive and appealing.

Phone
You can show this if you want to be easy to get a hold of (especially if you work in sales or consulting), or omit it if you prefer.

Address
Add in your address if clients visit you at your workplace. Or, if you're self-employed and work out of a home office, consider using my technique with this text which helps to show profile viewers where I'm based and which geographical areas I serve:

> *Based in Macomb County, Michigan, USA. Services provided throughout Michigan and online.*

Email
Only one email shows here, and it's the email you designate as "Primary" in your Settings & Privacy area.

First: Is the email shown accurate?

Next: If you're job seeking, I recommend using a home email (Gmail, etc.) as your primary email.

If you're employed and using LinkedIn for business development, your email should be your work email. *Why?* Because if I want to do business with you and see a Yahoo email listed here, I am going to feel odd emailing you at home with a business question. I'll tell myself I'll find your email "later" …but later never comes. Don't create a hurdle. Make it *easy* for people who want to do business with you.

Twitter

If you are ACTIVE on Twitter, include your Twitter handle here. See "Privacy & Settings" for instructions.

BONUS TIP: Your contact info is virtually hidden in the view of your profile on the mobile app. It's all the way at the bottom of your profile. For this reason, I encourage you to include some contact info (I have my email) in the first few lines of your About statement as well as in your Experience section for your current employer.

My favorite pie is pumpkin. I appreciate your marvelous presence on LinkedIn, thank you!
~ Al Dudley
www.linkedin.com/in/al-dudley-75622091

Chapter 24:

FEATURED & Media

*"When entrepreneurs are free to compete, they grow the
pie so that everyone's share gets larger."*
~ *John Stossel*

I don't know how to tell you this, so I'm just going to come out and say it:

Your LinkedIn profile can be boring. In fact, it might be boring right now.

After all, it's basically just a bunch of black and white text. Not knowing how to add color throughout your LinkedIn profile is like baking a pie with no added salt or sugar; it's bland. It may even look unappetizing.

Ever see a double crust pie with sprinkled sugar on top next to one that's plain? Or a pie that has been dressed with an egg wash versus one without? It's all about appearance, my friends.

We all know which pie looks more appealing: the one with the sugar or the shiny-looking crust. It just looks more delicious.

Similarly, there are several ways to add visual interest to your LinkedIn profile, and one way is by adding items to your FEATURED and media sections.

You can upload media into two areas of your profile: in your FEATURED section, as well as within each employer in your EXPERIENCE section.

I recommend you upload media to BOTH areas because it creates visual interest everywhere on your profile. Remember: your goal is to keep the RIGHT people on your profile for a longer time. Black and white text can be supplemented with media in the form of:

➤ Photos: jpegs or pngs.
➤ Videos: which you can link to on a YouTube or Vimeo channel.
➤ Work samples or marketing materials in the form of Word documents, PDFs, or PowerPoints. Or, any other items that are in those file formats.
➤ OR, you can point to website links. This could include videos, but it could also be blogs, web pages on your website, your portfolio link, event web pages, or even a LinkedIn post. Basically anything that has a web address can be added in.

PLUS: In the FEATURED section, which LinkedIn rolled out in early 2020, you can now showcase:

➤ Posts
➤ Articles (LinkedIn Blogs)

Do keep in mind a few items when selecting what to feature or when uploading media:

1. **Media is listed in the order in which it was added, with the latest upload / link listed at the left.** No, you cannot reorder these. You will have to delete and re-upload (or link) to re-order items. For this reason, make sure that the first 2-3 items are the prominent and that they are current. In other words, remove old event flyers or links.

2. **Featured items, however, CAN be reordered by a drag and drop.** I recommend the first two items in FEATURED are those with the greatest importance. The third item will be cut off, but still visual. And since the FEATURED items are huge on your profile when compared to media, they have greater visibility. Look at my profile in desktop and mobile view, and you'll see what I mean.

3. **Consider what is viewable. Remember, "people are lazy."** While I don't really think that people are *lazy*, this will help you to remember that most people won't click through or expand on images to see the big picture and caption. But the right people WILL if you've captured their attention. Look at the media / featured items on your profile in desktop view and mobile view. What do you notice? I notice that FEATURED is still visible even on mobile view. Well, at least the first few items. I'm looking at my profile in the mobile app right now, and I can see three thumbnails of media in my Featured section and then more than seven others denoting additional items which I can see if I click on them.

In contrast, any media I upload to my experience section isn't viewable on mobile unless I click to see the detail for each position. They are essentially tucked under an area of your profile which doesn't look like it expands (until you click on it and discover it does!). With about half of web traffic today occurring on mobile, that means about half of your audience can't see any media in your LinkedIn profile. Plus, you'd be safe to assume that most people won't click to expand your experience on mobile (because let's be honest: most won't).

I recommend you review this section and look at my profile at the same time. Unless you have media on your profile, this won't make a lot of sense.

One final note: delete media / featured if no longer relevant or if outdated. If you've included a flyer for a webinar you hosted in 2017 in your media section, I'm going to assume your profile isn't current.

4. **Be aware of the thumbnail preview**. LinkedIn only shows a portion of the image in thumbnail view. I've found multiple sites mentioning ideal dimensions for many items in LinkedIn, but I haven't found any sites that have given me the ideal dimensions for media you upload as a jpeg or png. My advice for you is to upload it in its original size first, then look at the uploaded media in desktop and mobile view. If you're not happy with it, you may need to try other dimensions. I follow the recommended ideal image size for a post which is 1200x628px, and it seems to work fine.

Keep in mind that the thumbnail is tiny, so consider how the image looks when viewing it. I like to see a variety of different images because it creates visual interest. I've seen other LinkedIn trainers who use a carefully designed branded thumbnail for brand consistency. There's no right or wrong way– but do be aware of your thumbnails and how they look.

On a related note, be aware that if you're pointing to a web page, LinkedIn will grab the image set by the web page for preview, and if there's not one set, it will grab the first image it can find on the web page. Sometimes this works, and other times, your preview looks like a gray icon because there is no image. Or, it's a logo that gets elongated or pixelated (yes, it's a word. And it contains the word PIE if you look closely).

When I'm pointing to a web page and there is no image or the image isn't loading properly and I'm not able to fix it on the web page, I may upload an image instead and put the web page link in the description of the media for the user to copy/paste. Consider that human beings are looking at your media, and try to make it as easy as possible for them to clearly see what you are trying to show.

As you upload items, you'll notice LinkedIn allows you to type in a title and description. The title pulls from the file name but it can – and usually should – be rewritten. The description sometimes gets filled in depending on the document or web page you're showing, but you can still override this here with manual text.

Be strategic about what shows, and look at your media in preview mode to see what others see.

What to show in Featured / Media?
Get creative! Think about items that support your goals in using LinkedIn.

You may wish to consider adding awards or career achievements, certificates completed, etc. in each "Media" section for each career you've held. This helps to show your career progression and expertise.

You can also look up your competitors or profiles of heavy LinkedIn users and you may be inspired with other ideas.

So, for example, after I looked up other presenters, I noticed that they have a speaker demo video (aka "sizzle reel") in their FEATURED section. Or, that they are promoting their book. BRILLIANT!

You can also upload sell sheets, product offers, or other marketing collateral (brochures, one-sheets, FAQs, etc.) in featured / media. Prospective clients visiting your profile (PLUS your sales and marketing team) will appreciate this.

My favorite pie is apple pie.
~ Vicente Romano
www.linkedin.com/in/vicenteromano

Section 4:

Invitation & Messaging Strategy

Chapter 25:

Invite Strategically and Build Dialog

"Historically, one of the seminal features of a pie is its ability to be eaten out of the hand."
~ *Janet Clarkson*

When you're getting started on LinkedIn, you learn many things from trial and error. Or by poking around the site. Or by asking friends and connections for their tips.

And sometimes LinkedIn gives you advice along the way. But following the default buttons to connect could actually slow your efforts in expanding your LinkedIn network.

I'm here to convince you how and why to personalize your invitation ("Add a Note" or "Personalize Invite"), and offer some tips on how to personalize it from either the desktop or the mobile app.

> **TIP: Skip the import step.**

Let's start at the beginning, when you first sign up for your LinkedIn account. There are several steps in the process: signing up, receiving a confirmation email, clicking the link to verify your account, and setting up your profile.

LinkedIn also offers you a quick and easy way to invite people to connect with you on LinkedIn: by inviting everyone in your email address book to connect. You may see an "import" button or something similar.

Personally, I never think it's a good idea to use this particular LinkedIn feature for several reasons:

There may be people in my email contact list whom I do NOT wish to invite to connect with me. For example, my Dad who is not and never will be on LinkedIn, my great aunt who would have no use for it, my friend whom I'm already connected with through his work email (so I wouldn't want to send him ANOTHER invitation to his personal email that's not on his LinkedIn account), etc.

If you follow the simple, step-by-step instructions, it will automatically send those individuals a LinkedIn invitation with no note. With the growing popularity of LinkedIn, you may receive dozens or even hundreds of "blind" invitations each week. And if you can't quite place the person who is inviting you to connect, you're likely to ignore it.

> **TIP: A personalized invitation is *ALWAYS* better than the standard invite. AKA "Optional" should not be *optional*.**

I always suggest that LinkedIn users take a few moments to personalize EVERY invitation. As in EVERY invitation. This includes EVERY invitation. (Yes, it's *that* important). How do you personalize an invitation, you ask? And did you really mean every one? YES. Every invitation, every time. I'm trying to break you of bad habits by creating positive new behaviors.

Start by visiting the person's profile (either desktop or mobile). NEVER send an invite from the LinkedIn suggestions list. If you click the "INVITE" button from either search results or from the suggestions list, it sends the invitation off without giving you the opportunity to personalize it.

At the end of 2019 I noticed that, sometimes, when you click "invite" from the connections list, the box pops up to ask if you'd like to send an invite.

However, I would rather not chance it. If you go to their profile, you're not at risk for missing that personalization opportunity.

> HINT: Most people *don't* personalize invites. The people who DO personalize have a higher chance of their invitations being accepted, especially if you are making that invitation all about the other person.

On desktop, there are two ways to send an invitation to a profile.

1. *Hit the "CONNECT" button.*

   Most profiles have "Connect" as the default button. Do you see this? Great. Click "connect" and then when you see the option to "Add a note" – click on it. This is the part where you can add the personalization. The formula I follow is:

If I know the person or if I've met them before:

Hi [first name], you may recall we met at [event / company… etc. add in context]. Let's connect on LinkedIn. [Your First Name / Last Name]

The more specific you can be (especially if there is a chance they won't remember you), the better. If it's someone you just met that day, less information is needed. But the key elements are:

➤ Greeting and use their name.
➤ Including context of how you know them.

➤ Request the invitation. "Let's connect on LinkedIn." Note that I always include "on LinkedIn" because I don't want them to think I'm asking them to meet for coffee or lunch or at an event.

➤ Your name.

The goal here is to get your invitation *accepted*.

If you're using LinkedIn for business development, your goal is not to sell to them in this stage, even if you want to *eventually* sell to them.

If you're a job seeker, your goal at this step is NOT to ask for a job, even if you want to ask them for a job you're applying for now or in the future.

For everyone else: your goal at this step is NOT to ask them for any favor, even if you want to ask them for a favor.

Show restraint for these items until – *if* – they accept your invitation. This is an element of online professional etiquette. Nobody wants to be sold to or asked for something in a LinkedIn invitation. You're building trust at this phase.

> LinkedIn success and social selling is a bit like dating. You wouldn't ask your blind date to marry you before the appetizers have arrived because, if you did, they would likely run away from the table and block your calls.
>
> You should get to know the person first. Show interest in them. Earn their trust. Ask them out on a second date. Meet their parents. Cook a meal for them. Spend a holiday together. Find out if they like pie and, if so, which kind.
>
> And then if all things seem right, *then* you ask them to marry you!

Same goes for LinkedIn. Get to know the person first. Show interest in them before trying to sell or ask them for anything. Earn their trust. Go slowly with your asks. Be polite. Be resourceful. Build social media karma. Pay it forward. And then, do your asking. At that point, they are more likely to want to buy from you or help you.

2. ***Not seeing the "CONNECT" button? Look for MORE and click the drop-down.*** You should now see 'Personalize invitation' as an option.

Some profiles – such as mine – have "FOLLOW" as the default button. This was set by the person whose profile you are viewing.

I've started to build up a large following and want to continue to grow my network, but I want my connections to be *intentional*. By setting "FOLLOW" as the default button, you can see my posts and updates.

Those people who really want to connect with you will take a minute to dig and find the "Connect" button, or they will send a message. Or, I might see that they have viewed my profile and I'll invite THEM to connect.

If you want to connect with accounts that show "FOLLOW" as the default, there is **usually** a way to do so. On their profile, click the three dots or the MORE button, and one of the menu options should read "Connect" or "Personalize invite." Click that and you should now have the option to "Add a note" to connect with the person.

Every now and again, you won't see any option to connect with a person or they'll have their account set up so that you need to add an email to connect with them. If you have their email, great. If not, just give them a follow, then comment on a recent post and like a post or two. By doing so, your name will start to become familiar to the person, and someday, they may invite you to connect. If not, move on. There are 722 million+ other people who may be easier to connect with!

3. **On mobile, the process to include a personal note or invitation text is a bit different.**

First, just like on desktop, you need to be ON the person's profile. You know you're in the right place when you can see their header graphic behind their headshot.

You need to be inside the LinkedIn app to do this. You can't be on a mobile version of the website on your phone. Now, click the "MORE" button or the three dots and you will find "Connect" or "Personalize Invite." Now, follow the same steps as before:

➤ Greeting.
➤ Mention if you've met them and, if so, where.
➤ If you haven't met them, refer to one or two items in their profile that are interesting to you, or that you have in common.

Again, *yes* this is worth the time it takes. Over time, you will become really efficient at this OR you may learn techniques to semi-personalize invitations to help optimize your time and effort for personalizing. More on this later in the SEARCH section.

IMPORTANT: Do not *sell* in the invitation. The invitation is not about you. It's about the other person.

ALSO IMPORTANT: Include something that indicates you didn't just copy and paste or send a mass invitation. (ex: "Since we are both professionals, let's connect on LinkedIn." = SPAMMY!)

So, let's say you've gone through all of this effort and the person has accepted your invitation.

BRAVO.

Now you're done and you can move onto the next connection, right?

WRONG.

This is where the fun really begins. Now, you want to take the next step in the conversation and keep the dialog going.

Remember my earlier analogy that doing business with someone on LinkedIn is a bit like dating? This part is similar to the back-and-forth conversation you have while enjoying an appetizer together.

Use the context of the invitation text to continue the dialog. Sometimes, you'll get lucky and the person will send YOU a message.

For example, sometimes when I connect with people on LinkedIn, I mention that we both attended Central Michigan University and I'll write "Fire up chips!" (our school slogan) in the invite. The person may write back and say, "Fire up chips! Have you been back to see campus lately?" Or something similar.

Now, I've got them talking. There's nothing more exciting than serving a piece of social media pie and the person accepting the pie and then thanking me for the pie.

Anyone else hungry for pie? No? Just me?

I would now reply back to the person and say something like, "I was on campus for 'Dialog Days' a few years ago and couldn't believe how different everything looked, but then again things seemed just the same while speaking in the classroom."

Just a bit of dialog can go a long way to establishing rapport, trust, and demonstrating that you are a real live human being just like them.

Some of my recent client engagements began with simple dialog exchanges like this, and I had to do ZERO cold calling to get them to talk with me.

At this point, I'll also thank the person for accepting my LinkedIn invitation, and offer a one- or two-line description of my business and tell them to keep me in mind if they'd like to learn more. Then I may ask them how they are using LinkedIn, and/or offer to be a resource for their business with my LinkedIn network.

There are two parts to this:

1. Here's what I'm selling, in case you're looking to buy this. A soft sell, and that's it. I don't add them to my eNews without permission (please don't do this, by the way). I don't ask to set up a coffee meeting or phone call. I don't send them a bunch of case studies or links. Ick. No.

2. I ask them how they are using LinkedIn (aka: what are YOU selling?). People really respect the fact that you're coming clean with what you're selling, but they also appreciate the fact that you're asking about THEIR business. It's creating a feeling of reciprocity (you help me, I help you) and we haven't even met yet.

3. Oh, and there's actually a third part. I may end with "have a great weekend!" or "have a wonderful day!" so the last part of the message isn't a sales message or an ask of them.

If they respond to this, then I take the conversation wherever it goes. If they never ask about my business again, that's fine with me.

"Wait, WHAT?," you may be thinking.

"I bought this book hoping you'd teach me how I can create sales through connections. And you don't care if they don't want to buy from you?"

Oh, yes, *I care*. But I know that they are now connected to me, so I can soft sell them every time I post on LinkedIn. If I'm posting interesting content, my posts will regularly appear in their homepage feed and, eventually, they will either message me back, or refer someone to me, or like or comment on a post, which then broadcasts out to THEIR network, and my name gets in front of more people.

It's a numbers game but it's weighted heavily on interesting content.

Remember these items:

1. The goal of sending an invitation is to get your invitation accepted. Not to sell in the invitation. Not to ask for anything in the invitation.

2. Always always always include a personal note in the invitation. Even on mobile.

3. Give the invitation some context to them. Use content from their profile that shows you've made an effort.

4. After they accept, keep the conversation going with a soft sell, an offer to help them, and a friendly closing.

5. If they don't accept, move on. There are plenty more people you can connect with in the future.

My favorite kind of pie is banana cream. What is yours?
~ Mike Weiss
www.linkedin.com/in/mikeweiss

Chapter 26:

LinkedIn Jail

Samantha: These <fast food apple pies>
are surprisingly delicious!
Carrie: I know! Why would anybody go to the trouble of
making one when you can buy one that is so
perfect and individually-sized?
~ Scene from "Sex and the City"

Back in October 2017, while reviewing business cards I collected from networking events I've attended, I received a message from LinkedIn when trying to send out an invitation to Kathy Mielke, a woman I met at *Inforum Troy.*

The message read:

> *"Do you know Kathy? To help keep LinkedIn a trusted community, we encourage members to only send invitations to people they know. You may soon be asked for the email address of members you invite as verification."*

Then, there was a "Learn more" link as well as a button to "Add a note" or "Send now."

It appeared I was nearing an invitation limit.

I wasn't able to determine what the "limit" of invitations was, nor was I required to add the email address of Kathy (though I have it on her business card).

I was curious if I was getting flagged by the LinkedIn police as I had been sending out a lot of invitations around that time, or if was for the total number of unaccepted invitations.

So, I did what any inquisitive and skilled LinkedIn member would do: I kept sending invitations until I reached my limit. And then I did some digging...

After a few more messages, I received a message saying I could no longer send invitations due to the total number of outstanding invitations.

There was a link to a page on LinkedIn about "Connecting with people you know and trust" which is kind of like being thrown into LinkedIn Jail where they hand you a pamphlet about what it means to be a *good* LinkedIn citizen.

I kinda broke LinkedIn, you guys. I was suddenly in LinkedIn "JAIL" which prohibited me from sending out any additional invites.

The average person might be frustrated. Me? I was thrilled!

I knew this would make for an interesting blog! And so I wrote about it.[13]

My next step was to see what LinkedIn had to say. While they didn't say what the limit was, they did provide instructions on how to view and withdraw any invitations I sent that weren't accepted yet. By reviewing my "sent" list, I determined the number of LinkedIn invitations you could have outstanding (unaccepted) is 250. Keep in mind, this was in 2017.

---

13 www.linkedin.com/pulse/linkedin-sent-invitations-limit-im-jail-least-month-brenda

Then, LinkedIn locks you up, throws you in jail, and requires you to input an email (as long as you're below 250 outstanding invitations). Nah, I'm just kidding. Well, at least about putting you in jail.

I figured out I needed to delete some unaccepted sent invites. I went to the oldest messages, which were at least a few months old. I deleted a few hundred that were not yet accepted so I don't have this problem again anytime soon.

As much as I would have liked to send out additional invites at the time, I couldn't. I had to wait a month before trying to send any new invitations to connect.

After my limit of sending out new invites had been lifted (aka, I was "released from LinkedIn Jail"), I could send out additional invites.

However, I was still on "probation" for the month, requiring me to input an email address before sending any other invites. During this month, I ate a LOT of pie. (I'm kidding.)

It appears the pending invitation limit has changed over time. At the time of this writing, I have 190 pending connection requests with the oldest pending invite 11 months ago, leading me to conclude invites still pending after 12 months are deleted by LinkedIn.

The items that will put you into LinkedIn Jail seem to be changing over time, but here's what I've learned from my own activities and those of my clients that have landed us in jail. And keep in mind I'm sharing this list with you to keep you focused on the RIGHT activities, not to give you the playbook to hack LinkedIn.

1. **Do NOT use any automated services for sending out bulk invitations**. If you do so, you are violating LinkedIn's terms of service. Their tech team is getting smarter at detecting this and

you will eventually get caught. The first time you may get a warning and be put into 'jail.' If you keep repeating this, you'll eventually get your invitation privileges permanently revoked. Yes, I heard this happened to someone after their third time using automated tools for sending bulk invites.

2. **Be a real person.** LinkedIn is getting better at identifying spammy accounts or accounts that are not real people. For this reason, I do not recommend you set up a business page on a personal profile (or a mascot or anything else).

3. **Don't think you can use LinkedIn as a replacement for eHarmony.** Go to eHarmony for those purposes.[14]

If you do land in LinkedIn jail for some other reason, contact me and I'll see if I can help. No promises, but since I'm a heavy user on LinkedIn, I might be able to offer you guidance.

My favorite pie is Apple Pie from Donaldson's Farm in NJ.
~ Jeannie Wong
www.linkedin.com/in/jeanniecwong

---

14   See also: www.linkedin.com/pulse/women-linkedin-responding-unprofession
al-message-meller-zawacki-

Chapter 27:

Three-Step Messaging Strategy

[On tasting Rachel's English trifle/Shepherd's pie]
Ross: It tastes like feet!
Joey: I like it!
Ross: Are you serious?
Joey: What's not to like?
Custard, good. Jam, good. Beef, GOOD!
~ Scene from 'Friends'

If you are using LinkedIn for business development and/or to sell to people, we need to have a talk. Sure, you may be awesome at selling. You might even be the top producer at your company for the past 20 years. You may have won awards, trips, or even that Barbie Jeep for your kids when they were little.

But if you're using LinkedIn to try to sell to people, you might be going about it entirely wrong.

> **DO ANY OF THESE POINTS DESCRIBE YOU?**
> ➤ I include my contact info, a calendar link, a link to our product demo, or information about my company's product (or services) in an invitation to connect.

> ➤ I send blank invitations to my prospects, and then as soon as they accept, I include my contact info, a calendar link, a link to our product demo, or information about my company's product (or services) in an invitation to connect.
>
> ➤ As soon as someone connects with me, I grab their email and add it to my email list so they receive future email newsletters from my company. OR, I immediately send a one-to-one email with an overview of my products or services to their email.
>
> ➤ After someone connects with me, I send them periodic articles that prove my products (or services) are something they need, even if they never respond.
>
> If any of the above points describe you, then please stop immediately. *Seriously*.

A bunch of us were talking about you and it's annoying. The chances of us wanting to do business with you are pretty slim. In fact, sometimes we compare notes about what you said.

True story: I once received an email from a man who worked for a financial planning company who said I was connected to his dad on LinkedIn (I was not, nor was I connected to him) and he said something along the lines of, "since you're getting old, you need to think about your retirement savings and I can help."

It was really not that far off from what his email said. *Really*.

Yes, we are all getting older. No, I don't need you to remind me.

But let's get back to the three-step messaging strategy. If you are using LinkedIn to try to find prospects and sell to them, please go a bit slower. Pitching me on your products or services before we've even had a chance to get to know each other online is like me going on a blind date with you, and you proposing marriage before the appetizers arrive.

Want to sell more effectively to your new connections on LinkedIn? Slow down. Get to know them. Demonstrate proper etiquette. Have patience.

Here's what I suggest and why:

STEP 1: Send them an invitation to connect, and make the invitation ALL ABOUT THEM. Do not sell in your invitation. Do not ask for a call or coffee meeting. Do not push any of your company information on them.

Your goal when sending an invitation is to get that invitation accepted. It's not to sell.

You have a better likelihood that your invitation will be accepted if it includes a personal note that demonstrates to the other person that you've taken a minute or two to look at their profile.

Don't use an automated response that shows no personalization at all, such as:

"You have an impressive profile. Let's connect!"

"Because you're someone I trust, I'd like to connect with you on LinkedIn."

"I'm interested in growing my connections network with great specialists and influencers. I'm co-founder of a [industry type] company. We specialize in [products and services]. Looking forward to possibly working with you."

"Would you be open to connecting? We've got some contacts in common, your profile caught my eye and I thought it would be interesting to make a connection with other coaches."

"Congratulations on all of your success. I'm an entrepreneur from [city that is not my city]. Would love to connect with you here."

"I am a seller for Fiverr. Your website sells and promoted the best way of my service. My services worldwide promote your website. Can I help you? My Services Link: (link) So, please place your order. I guaranteed you will be glad."

"It seems like we know some of the same people. I am always looking to expand my network, and when I came across your profile I thought it would be good to connect. Please accept my invitation."

Because LinkedIn is rising in popularity, there is also a rise in LinkedIn "helper" tools where you can input your target audience criteria, and then send out hundreds of invitations per hour.

Sounds appealing, right? It's too good to be true.

Use of these tools violates LinkedIn's terms of service. And if LinkedIn discovers you are using automated tools, they will freeze your account. If you keep doing it, you will be banned from sending new invites via LinkedIn, and you could even lose the ability to access LinkedIn altogether.

That's not a risk I will take with my account. It's not worth it. The mass approach isn't as successful as a personal approach.

On a related note, over the past few years I have had several LinkedIn "coaches" reach out to me to offer help with my LinkedIn profile. It was obvious they didn't take even a minute to look at my profile before inviting me to connect, and I messaged them back with a simple response: "Is this an automated invite?" Most of them ignored me.

A personal invitation is all about them, and it informs them if you have met or not, something you have in common or that's interesting to you that you read on their profile, and the only reason for reaching out is to connect. That's it. *Simple.*

Like an apple pie with homemade ingredients. You simply cannot produce homemade in mass. Homemade pie is better than mass assembly line pie that is shoved full of preservatives. It is simply better quality.

STEP 2: After they accept your invitation, reply by thanking them for connecting. Include a one-line description of your products / services. Perhaps ask them how you can be a referral connection for them.

Something like this:

> *Thanks for accepting my invite, Brad. My business is Meller Marketing https://www.linkedin.com/company/meller-marketing-llc/ and I specialize in helping people and companies unlock the power of LinkedIn. Let me know if I can ever be a resource for you.*
>
> *And if you have a minute, tell me how I can help leverage my LinkedIn network to help you. Brenda Meller*

Notice here that I haven't included any external links or contact info outside of LinkedIn. This is as sales-y as I get on LinkedIn, unless a person expresses interest in learning more. If you never respond, this is where my messaging ends with you until you reach back out to me.

STEP 3: If they respond, continue the dialog. This step does not occur with every new connection, and to be honest, it's probably a small percentage, but when it does happen, it's magical.

If they do respond, you have dialog. This is awesome! Now you're different than the thousands of other people they have connected on LinkedIn.

A response back is an indication that you have passed their criteria for continuing the conversation. My advice at this point is to match their reply back to you. If they comment on something in your message, keep the conversation going as long as it feels natural. Don't be pushy and don't be sales-y.

I am a marketer, not a salesperson, but this approach is effective in building genuine dialog that enhances your professional relationships by establishing trust.

End the conversation when it comes to a natural end. This is not a three-step process to selling. This is just the beginning.

Now that they are connected with you, they are going to see your posts. Eventually, a portion of these people will like (or react to) your posts, or add a comment.

Now that they are connected with you, you may wish to visit their profile and like or comment on a few of their recent posts. Then, walk away. Don't be a stalker or someone who looks overly enthusiastic and likes all ten of their latest posts. Yes, we notice and it's odd.

Give this approach a try, and let me know your results by sending me a message on LinkedIn. And if you've had other overly-aggressive sales pitches on LinkedIn, know that you're not alone and I'm trying to get to everyone to tell them to stop.

Hoping to connect - as my favorite pie is pecan.
~ Michael Gregory
www.linkedin.com/in/michael-gregory-97bab33

Chapter 28:

Have We Met?
Screening Invitations to Create Dialog

JERRY: (still talking to George) I'm sorry. There's no reason for her not to taste that pie.
ELAINE: Who wouldn't taste a pie?
JERRY: Audrey.
ELAINE: Dump her.
JERRY: Boy, I never broke up with anyone for not tasting pie???
ELAINE: (piffling) I once broke up with someone for not offering me pie.

~ Scene from 'Seinfeld'

Let's talk about invitations you receive from people you don't know on LinkedIn and who did not include a personal note. What do you do with those invitations? Here are the common responses I hear from clients:

"If I don't know them, I ignore or decline them. I only connect with people I know."

"If they aren't from a country where I do business, I decline or archive them."

"I look at their profile and make a judgement call on whether or not I think they would be a good fit to connect with or if they look like they are going to sell to me."

"I look and see who we have in common."

"I accept ALL invitations. I'm a LION (LinkedIn Open Networker)."

"If we haven't met or have never talked, I don't accept."

"I only connect with people I know really well."

"I click 'I don't know this person.'"

All of the above are perfectly fine responses, and there is no one right or wrong answer. However, you are reading this book because you want to make LinkedIn work better for you, *right*?

> It's time for some tough love: STOP DECLINING ALL INVITATIONS WITH ARBITRARY CRITERIA BASED ON YOURSELF.
>
> There may be a reason someone sent you an invitation to connect on LinkedIn, and unless you've asked the person for clarification, you'll never know.

Sure, some of the invitations you receive are like junk mail: they're sent out to everyone without any personal connection.

Some invitations are the results of LinkedIn suggesting your profile to people to connect with, where they simply click the "Connect" button when LinkedIn suggests it.

If LinkedIn suggests it, there's probably a reason, right? *WRONG*.

LinkedIn's goal is to increase your time on the site and increase connections you make because the more people you connect with, the more often you're on the site and the more ads they can serve you, the more potential for you to upgrade to Premium, etc.

Don't get me wrong. I think LinkedIn is AMAZING and I spend a LOT of time on the site. But my invitation requests and consideration of requests sent to me are all intentional.

This is one of my secrets of my own LinkedIn success, and now I'm going to share it with you.

First, let's all assume that people are sending you invitations to connect on LinkedIn with no knowledge that there is a way to include a personal note. Or, they see the option from LinkedIn but LinkedIn says it's "optional," so why bother? Or, there is no option to include a personal note because the invitation was sent as soon as you clicked connect. Or, they don't understand the value of a personal note.

Regardless of the reason: it's not intentional. They just don't know any better.

But this does provide YOU with an opportunity to create dialog by replying to the invitation sender and including a message. Screen every invitation in and create dialog.

Follow these steps to give this a try:

➤ To do so, go into the desktop version of LinkedIn. Click on "My Network" in the top menu bar. If you have any pending invitations, you'll see these in a list.
➤ On this page (*www.linkedin.com/mynetwork*), click on "See all 70" or whatever your number of pending invitations is. This text link is in the upper right hand of your screen, just above the most recent invitation you've received.

- ➤ When you click on this, it will take you to a similar-looking page (*www.linkedin.com/mynetwork/invitation-manager*), but now underneath every invitation, you'll see the link, "Message." You now have the ability to message these people before deciding whether or not to accept an invitation.
- ➤ Click on "Message" and a box will appear to send this person a message from you.

"BUT BRENDA," you are thinking, "WHAT DO I *SAY* IN THE MESSAGE?"

I'm so glad you asked. Try this short version:

> *Hi [first name]. Thanks for the LinkedIn invitation. Have we met? [Your Name]*

Now, I *know* we haven't met. And *they* know we haven't met. But it's more polite to message this, rather than to say, "Who the heck are you and why do you want to connect with me?"

Basically, the message is saying the same thing, but it's more polite and professional.

What I've found is that the INTENTIONAL invitation people will respond. These are the individuals who sent you an invitation *on purpose*. Maybe they visited your profile. Maybe they met you at an event. Maybe someone suggested your profile. Whatever the case, they will typically respond within a few business days with clarification if their invitation was intentional.

Voilà! Now you have a dialog to continue the conversation. If you hadn't screened them in, you would have made a decision based on your past (arbitrary) system for reviewing invitations, and I guarantee you've missed out on some good opportunities for networking, and possibly even some business referrals.

I also have a long version, if you're feeling even more courageous and bold. I'm happy to share this with you and I'm totally fine if you want to use it for yourself:

> Hi [first name], Thanks for the invitation to connect on LinkedIn. I look forward to connecting.
>
> I screen in every connection using this technique, which has started some great conversations with people from around the world.
>
> Perhaps we have met in person. If so, can you help to remind me where? I'm having a hard time recalling. This gets a bit trickier the more networking events I attend.
>
> If we haven't met, could you clarify why you sent me an invite? Most often, I hear that LinkedIn suggested me, but occasionally people say they visited my profile or saw a helpful status update from me or where I was tagged. I'm open to connecting - just curious what prompted you to reach out.
>
> I am open to connecting with you and I look forward to your response. Brenda Meller

A few notes on this before we go any further...

I caution you to make sure that this fits your voice and describes how *you* are using LinkedIn. You want to be truthful and honest.

I have had a few people ask me if this is automated (it's not), and I share that it's a template I save on my desktop– but I do use it with every new invitation. I save this in my notepad for easy reference, and so it removes the web coding that LinkedIn adds into invitation messages.

I have had a few (very few: maybe 3-5 people) complain it's too long to read and they refuse to respond. That's perfectly fine with me. Keep in mind they included no personal note to me when they sent me an invitation to connect. And they sent ME the invite.

They are the ones who are doing the asking, and I'm under no obligation to connect with them.

And to be perfectly honest, if you can't be bothered to read a long message back from me – or to even skim it to understand my point – we probably wouldn't make good connections for each other anyway.

I once had a senior executive reply that he was offended with my long message, and he tried to educate me on how to use LinkedIn properly. He mentioned he had decades of experience with networking and I was going about it all wrong.

I replied that I appreciated his response, and asked him to specify what it was about my message that offended him. I listened to his feedback and reduced a bit of the text, but reiterated to him that this approach was very effective for me. No, we did not connect.

But, yes, I did create dialog with him and that was my only goal with this message.

Create dialog. It's magical.

By creating dialog with your new invitation requestors, you break yourself out from the clutter of the hundreds and thousands of people who invite you to connect on LinkedIn.

You become human. *Real.* A genuine person and a connection are created. Not just a LinkedIn connection, but a *human* connection.

It's the same thing that happens when I bring a pie to give away at an event, and I ask a few attendees to share their favorite pie with me in our introductions.

I am breaking away from what's expected by creating dialog that is unexpected and welcome. This is one of the key essences of social media pie, in my opinion.

It's not welcome by everyone, but I guarantee it does help to reveal people's motives, character, and sometimes their values. If these don't line up with your goals, it saves you the time and connection with someone who won't really be a good connection.

If you read my short response and my long response, you'll notice that they both essentially say the same thing: *who are you and why do you want to connect with me?*

Give the other person a chance to respond, and you may be pleasantly surprised.

Try this for a week and see what happens.

Now, some people never respond, and that's OK. If they don't reply, then I look at their profiles. I make a quick judgement call as to whether:

1. They would make a good connection for me to do business with.

2. They would make a good referral opportunity for me at some point in the future.

If the profile looks fake, inactive, or the person's activity (comments in particular) are unprofessional or don't align with my values, I ignore the invitation; I might also click, "I don't know this person." I do so because if the person gets several of these responses to their invitations, LinkedIn will message them with a reminder of the rules for connecting with others.

I used to accept every invitation at this point, as long as none of the above were apparent to me when I viewed their profile. My approach has since changed.

As my network continues to grow, I have started to become more selective about people I accept invitations from. As of today, I have over 16,000 connections. The current LinkedIn connection limit is 30,000. Since I'm over the halfway point, I've started to be a bit more focused on who would be a *good* connection.

If I don't feel it's a good fit (typically due to geographic area: I'm focused mainly on clients in Metro Detroit and in the U.S.), I reply with this message instead:

> *Thanks for the invitation to connect on LinkedIn. If you visit my profile on LinkedIn https://www.linkedin.com/in/brendameller, click the FOLLOW button and you'll receive my updates and tips.*
>
> *Thanks!*
>
> *Brenda Meller*

NOTE: I don't recommend everyone use this approach, especially if you're not active on LinkedIn (posting regularly), if your default button is CONNECT instead of follow, and if you're not posting updates or tips. But this has helped me to screen people into two categories:

➤ People I want to connect with, and
➤ People who may be interested in my content (but may not line up with my target audience).

Hopefully, the explanations and my approach provided here gives you some food for thought as you consider how to handle your pending invites on LinkedIn.

The last thing I'd like to mention here is: keep up with your invitations! Try to reply the same day or at least once a week to all your pending invitations.

My favorite pie is sweet potato pie.
~ Angel Hartfield
www.linkedin.com/in/angelhartfield

Section 5:

Network Engagement & Homepage Feed

Chapter 29:

Build Social Media Karma

When you die, if you get a choice between going to regular heaven or pie heaven, choose pie heaven. It might be a trick, but if it's not, mmmmmmmm, boy.
~ Jack Handy

As I sat down to pick what chapter of my book to write tonight, I showed my daughter Charlotte my book outline and asked her to pick the topic. She said, "build social media karma."

She probably picked it because it sounded interesting. I think we've talked about karma before, so it sounded familiar to her.

This chapter is going to reveal to you one of my biggest learnings to-date that's propelled my LinkedIn efforts to a whole other level: building social media karma.

One of the biggest mistakes I see people making on LinkedIn is that they focus on selling themselves, their business, their product, their services, their clients, or other items.

Want LinkedIn to work for you? You've got to focus on building social media karma.

The benefits of building social media karma reminds me of a story that involves my son, Joshua. A few years ago, we set him up at our credit union with his own savings account. They issued him a debit card for the account, and he was thrilled.

"Cool!" he said. "Now I can go shopping!"

I had to explain to Joshua that it doesn't work that way. You have to put money IN in order to be able to SPEND out of the account.

The same goes for LinkedIn. If you want to gain the benefits of using LinkedIn, you have to make deposits into your network.

The difference here is that you're making deposits in the form of social media karma rather than making a monetary deposit.

Yes, it takes effort. Yes, it takes time. No, you are not making this effort with any expectation that anyone is going to return the favor. *But they will*. It's just human behavior.

I once volunteered at TEDxDetroit and helped work backstage to coordinate moving speakers from the green room to the microphone set-up area. I helped to block non-VIPs from entering the stage area. I helped guide VIP guests, media, and general admission attendees to where they needed to go.

It was my first time working as a volunteer and Larry Miller (www.linkedin.com/in/connectedgeek) helped to guide me through my duties for the day. Larry's an experienced TEDxDetroit volunteer, and he's earned the stage duties to prove it– including donning a cool headset.

Around 2 p.m., as the end of my volunteer shift was approaching, I was chatting with Larry, and we both were tired from a long day. I think Larry arrived around 7 a.m. He mentioned he really needed some caffeine, and a Coke sounded really good. I told him I'd go find him one and returned a few minutes later, Coke in hand. He was delighted.

I didn't do this for any reason other than to make Larry smile. He was a hard-working volunteer and he was going to be there the rest of the day. I know how a bit of caffeine can give you the boost you need to help you push through when your energy is zapped.

I didn't expect Larry to return the favor, but I know I made an impression on Larry that he'll remember the next time he sees me post something on LinkedIn– and he might be more inclined to give my post a like or to leave a comment.

You, dear reader, have the power to make Larry and others in your network happy too.

Do what I do: spend 15 minutes in your homepage feed every single business day. Scroll through, and add a "LIKE" or other reaction to posts that resonate with you, or to posts made by people you know. Sure, you can add a different reaction like the 'applause' icon, but a simple 'like' goes a long way.

After you've liked a few posts, take another minute to find a post where you can leave a comment. When you comment, make sure the comment includes five words or more.

WHY? The algorithm.

Each network has an algorithm running behind the scenes. It determines which posts you will see when you visit your homepage feed. It also determines how long a post will stay there, and how many people will see the post.

I've learned – both from experience and from fellow LinkedIn connections – a few techniques that can help to generate more views for your posts.

First, keep in mind what appeals to people.

As human beings, we like making connections with other human beings. When I post something on LinkedIn, it's nice to see people liking or commenting on my post. When someone says "nice article!" it genuinely makes me smile.

However, if someone else says, "this is a great point and it reminds me of my favorite manager Keith who…", then I can tell that the message I posted really resonated with that person. I made a real connection with them and I know they took time to reply. Five or more words can go a long way toward demonstrating that we care.

Then, keep in mind the technology that runs on LinkedIn– or, the algorithm.

LinkedIn and other social networking sites have a goal. That goal is to keep you on their sites longer. If you see posts that have a higher likelihood of generating your engagement (likes, comments, shares), you will stay on LinkedIn longer.

Posts with comments of five or more words earn a higher rating by the algorithm, which keeps your post in the homepage feed longer and shows that post to more people.

The longer you stay on LinkedIn, the more ads they can serve you. Plus, you'll connect with more people, engage with more users, and create more content.

If all LinkedIn shows you are posts that aren't interesting to you, then you will likely spend less time on LinkedIn and leave quickly.

Remember the "trade show effect" I talked about earlier?

The same thing happens with a LinkedIn post. When you see a post that is generating lots of likes and comments, you are intrigued. You want to see what people are talking about and you might even feel inclined to join in on the conversation. You may notice that some of the people who commented look familiar, and you start interacting with their comments, too.

The more of THESE posts that LinkedIn serves to you, the longer you'll stay on LinkedIn.

That's great if that's your post, but what if it's someone in your network and you're helping to make that post more popular by adding a comment?

BONUS for that person! Plus, they see that you're someone commenting on their post. This makes them feel good. They may like your comment, or even add a comment back to thank you.

Do this a few times, and you've quickly elevated yourself to the top of that person's mindset. They will remember you, and perhaps they may even take a moment to visit your profile to view some of your recent posts.

Or, they may just make a mental note to thank you the next time they see you in-person.

Or, your comments may be helping to demonstrate your expertise, and the next time they come across someone needing your services, they'll immediately think of you.

You, my friend, have been making social media deposits into their account, and that person now wants to return the favor.

Do this a few times a week, and you'll see what I mean. No, the results won't happen right away. Yes, it takes time and effort.

Even if you just spend 15 minutes a week liking posts and commenting on 2-3 posts per week with comments of five or more words, you will notice a difference in a short period of time.

My favorite pie is cherry.

~ Jean Roth
www.linkedin.com/in/jean-roth

Chapter 30:

Checking Your Nets

Jim: Laverne packs up the pie wagon at five so...
Kevin: At five? That's only twenty minutes from now. The
pie shop is thirteen miles away. So at fifty-five miles an
hour that just gives us five minutes to spare.
Angela: So wait, when pies are involved you can
suddenly do math in your head?
Kevin: We...
Oscar: Hold on. Kevin, how much is 19,154 pies divided
by 61 pies?
Kevin: 314 pies.
Oscar: What if it were salads?
Kevin: Well, it's the... Carry the four... And... It doesn't work.
~ The Office TV show

Linkedin can offer you and your business a HUGE amount of opportunities, and some are literally right in front of your eyes. After I explain this concept to you, you won't be able to unsee it, and you'll probably want to send me a pie to say thank you!

The concept I'm going to explain to you now is *checking your nets*.

It's an analogy but one that I think will help you to really understand the opportunities you are creating and those that are waiting for you.

At the beginning of the day, a fisherman throws out a net into the sea to catch fish for the day. At the end of the day, he or she pulls in the net to see what they've caught.

Some of what gets caught in the net is garbage– literal trash collected by the net.

Some of what's caught includes fish that are too small, inedible, or undesirable.

But then, there's the bounty: the glorious catch of the day!

I know very little about fishing and this story may have some flaws in it. At any rate, it helps you to visualize the process. A net is used to catch fish. And you only get to enjoy the fish if you check your nets.

When I first meet with a client, I do a quick scan of their profile, and then their activity feed. Then, I look at their business page and the business page's activity feed. You know what I see? A LOT of caught fish.

When you post on LinkedIn, you are essentially casting a net to your network. The *post* is the *net* here: if it's a proper net, it will catch fish.

If the holes in the net are too large– well, that's like a sales pitch. Nobody will get caught because everyone can see a sales pitch coming and they avoid it.

If the net is too small, the fish swim right past it. That's the equivalent of posting once a month or just that one time six months ago.

If the post is just right (anyone else thinking about the Three Little Bears right now?), it will catch fish in the form of likes (or other reactions) and comments.

What makes a post *just right*?

➤ It educates, informs, or inspires.
➤ It appeals to your ideal target audience.
➤ It causes people to stop, read it, and interact with your post.
➤ It is done with some regularity. I recommend once every business day on your personal LinkedIn profile, and about 2-3 times per week minimum on your business page.

So, let's say you do all these things correctly. Then you're definitely catching fish in the form of network engagement (likes / reactions, comments, and shares).

By the way, shares of your posts are a whole other level of fishing. That's like when the fish are telling other fish to get in the net, and the other fish believe the first fish, because everybody believes their peers more than they do the source. The concept here is that of social proof.

I can offer you LinkedIn tips and tell you I provide LinkedIn strategy coaching and team training, but a part of you will feel like I'm selling to you and you'll tune me out.

But if someone in your network – someone you respect – raves about how awesome you are on LinkedIn and how you helped their team get active on LinkedIn, *well,* you'll believe them. If someone thinks this of me, and then you look up my profile, you'll see my contact info and reach out and ask me for a "virtual coffee" to "pick my brain." And before you know it, you've signed up to work with me and you're posting on LinkedIn to share techniques you've learned from me.

This is checking the nets. I'm going to leave this analogy and shift the talk to *engagement* on LinkedIn.

Let's say you are creating great engagement on your posts. You need to act on that engagement.

Look at every single person who likes – or *reacts* to – your post. If there's anyone who is not a first-level connection, consider sending them an invitation to connect, but don't mention them liking the post. They'll figure out why and they'll be impressed. You don't need to remind them.

Now, look at the comments. Every comment you've been given is a gift. When we receive a gift, we send a thank you note. On LinkedIn, you should do this in the form of a comment back to them, using five or more words.

Then, if they are not a first-level connection, invite them to connect. Again, do not mention their comment unless it was a meaningful exchange. They will remember you from the exchange and they don't need you to remind them.

Every post creates opportunities for you, and the beauty is that you don't have to chase after these opportunities. These opportunities come to you.

Take a moment to look at your activity feed right now.

You can even look at MY activity feed right now:

www.linkedin.com/in/brendameller/detail/recent-activity/shares

For that matter, you can look up the activity feed of your coworkers, your competitors, your vendors, your suppliers, your managers, people you admire, the head of LinkedIn, celebrities, etc. etc. The list goes on and on.

There are also opportunities on every single one of your company page posts. In fact, I recommend to my clients that they assign a salesperson to invite people to connect as a part of their lead generation activities.

There are opportunities all over the activity feed if you know where to look for it.

And consider this: people who are interacting with a post are interested in its content. For that reason, try looking up posts with certain hashtags too.

Oh, and don't tell your competition I told you this. After all, my goal is to support YOU, not them. (*See?* I do like you!)

Simple and brilliant, isn't it?

My favorite pie is pumpkin.
~ Greg Fratz
www.linkedin.com/in/gregfratz

Chapter 31:

Posting Strategy: Timing and Content

Moira: I would like two apple fritters, sliver of pecan pie, large fries with gravy and bacon!
Alexis: Okay, so, she will have scrambled egg whites and some steamed spinach, please, thank you.
Moira: And some pecan pie! Onion rings, and ice cream!
Alexis: Actually, none of that, and I will have a tea, thank you.
~ Schitt's Creek TV Show

Now that you've got an optimized profile on LinkedIn, you're one-third of the way to truly unlocking the power of this amazing platform.

"Wait a minute… a THIRD?!?," you exclaim, "but I'm more than halfway done with the book!"

That's because your profile is one of the single most important elements of your LinkedIn presence. If your profile is not optimized and accurate, all the traffic you'll be driving TO your profile from invitations, posts, and network engagement will be for naught.

It would be like setting up a marketing campaign and driving people to your retail location for a purchase, but the lights are burnt out, the door sticks when it opens, and there's empty pie tins mysteriously scattered outside the front door.

At any rate, let's shift focus from your profile (where you sell) to your homepage feed where you post (*and tell*).

Remember: Your profile is for SELLING and your posts are for TELLING. I first heard this expression from John Espirian. John is a relentlessly helpful technical copywriter based in the UK. (www.linkedin.com/in/johnespirian)

First, here's some data I want you to keep in mind when you are posting on LinkedIn.

As of today, LinkedIn says there are 722 million LinkedIn members[15].

However, we're not all on LinkedIn all the time. But when we are on, we're ON. We don't "hang out" on LinkedIn as we do on Facebook or Instagram.

The average user logs into LinkedIn and does his or her business before leaving the site.

It's like reading a newspaper: you pick it up, read it from cover to cover, then put it down.

According to Omnicore[16], just 48% of LinkedIn users visit LinkedIn once a month or more. That means HALF of your connections aren't even on LinkedIn once a month. Therefore, if you aren't posting regularly, you're missing people when they DO visit LinkedIn.

Plus, according to Buffer[17] (who cited LinkedIn but I'm unable to find the original data), if you post a status update on LinkedIn EVERY BUSINESS

---

15   Source: *about.linkedin.com/*
16   Source: *www.omnicoreagency.com/linkedin-statistics/*
17   Source: *buffer.com/library/social-media-frequency-guide*

DAY for a month, you will reach 60% of your first-level connections. That means that posting frequency is also very important.

> Due to these facts, I recommend you post on LinkedIn **once every business day.**
>
> Do this effectively and you will:
>
> ➤ Position yourself as a thought leader.
> ➤ Be top of mind for referrals, when someone in your network needs your service.
> ➤ Create a regular cadence of information for your network and your profile will become a destination for these insights.
> ➤ Enjoy a delicious slice of homemade pie.
> ➤ Win the lottery and move to Maui.
>
> OK, well maybe the last two aren't true. But I like to think that being effective on LinkedIn is the equivalent of enjoying a delicious slice of pie... or, basking in the sunlight in a tropical paradise, fruity drink in hand.

"But Brenda," you ask, "when is the best time of day to post?"
Well, that depends on who you're trying to reach and when they are most likely online. If you're not sure, think about your own activities and when YOU go onto LinkedIn.

It's likely first thing in the morning (either before you begin work), around the lunch hour, just before you leave work for the day, or after dinner and before you go to sleep.

I typically recommend posting early in the day when possible, but test out different times of day and days of the week to assess what works best.

I've recently experimented posting on the weekend, and I've had some really nice responses to Sunday night posts.[18]

What is more important than WHEN you post, however, is WHAT you post.

Here are my suggestions for WHAT to post on LinkedIn.

Keep in mind your goal with posts on LinkedIn is to do MORE TELLING and LESS SELLING to your network.

1. **Tell us about conferences, workshops, or other events you've attended.** This one is *so easy* once you get the hang of it. Every time you attend a professional event, make sure you snap a few photos of the presenter, keynote speaker, or even follow attendees. I personally like to stage my photos so the host organization's banner or logo appears in the photo, but that's the marketer in me.

   WHAT TO SAY IN YOUR POST:

   Today I attended the @(organization name) (event) at (location) in (City, State). If you're active in the (industry type) industry, I highly recommend checking out their upcoming events. It was great to see @(name of person1 in photo), @(name of person2 in photo), and many others.

   I'll be attending their (event name) next month. Reply below if you plan to attend too.

   BONUS: Include in the post a few of your key takeaways that you will be applying in your role.

---

18   Like this one: www.linkedin.com/posts/brendameller_linkedin-is-only-for-job -seekers-comment-activity-6601883347792777216-lKCs
And this one:
www.linkedin.com/posts/brendameller_linkedin-activity-6599407274962272256-3jyl

2. **When you are reading an online article about your industry, click to share it on LinkedIn.** Add a one-sentence description about what you learned by reading this article. This is a great way of multi-tasking. You are learning and sharing at the same time.

It reminds me of school when you would have to summarize a book in one or two sentences. When I share an industry article, I will always include one or two of my key takeaways. This helps ME focus on what I learned and, by sharing it with my network, it demonstrates my passion for the subject and my growing expertise.

3. **Share news, a press release, or even blogs from your personal LinkedIn page (aka LinkedIn articles) or from your company website.** Make sure the news is public before doing so, but certainly anything on your company's public website or even your company's LinkedIn company page is fair game to be shared.

I always like to include a one-sentence preview of what the link is pointing to, so my readers know what I'm sharing. I don't know about you, but I don't click the link unless I know it will be worth my time.

4. **Share business tips.** Say you're an expert in blogging. Share a few tips about what makes an effective blog. Or perhaps you're an expert in making coffee. I definitely would read those tips. Probably while drinking coffee. Or maybe the best places for pie because you're a foodie.

Chances are, you know more than the rest of us about something in your business that will be useful to other LinkedIn members.

Kareem George (www.linkedin.com/in/kareemgeorge) is a travel expert and he highlights exotic destinations, like this one: www.linkedin.com/posts/kareem-george-cta-6978922b_your spaceinthesun-antiguaandbarbuda-caribbeanparadise-activi ty-6720779102393122816-FCS0

Brilliant!

Here is an example of a post I do on #TakeActionTuesday, where my post features tips for those in career transition or those looking to hire. www.linkedin.com/posts/brendameller_meller-marketing-tips -for-stealth-job-search-activity-6610152664707719168-J3AA

5. **Tell us how we can help you.** Whereas all of the above points have been more storytelling than selling, this one is OK to be a direct pitch for your business. Remind your network of what you do and who you can help and how you can help them. Don't rely on your network to remember what you do. That's your job.

Even better, include a video clip, like I've done here youtu.be/ 1RKaeOKzjco Yes, it was a selfie video with no rehearsal. Thanks to Keith Stonehouse (www.linkedin.com/in/keithstonehouse) for the inspiration.

I just started talking. Guess what? This video led to a few business inquiries for Meller Marketing.

6. **Post a #FridayShout feature** of a fellow LinkedIn connection and give them a shout-out, as I've done here: www.linkedin.com/feed/update/urn:li:activity:64209628558 01102336 (for Terry Bean)

And here:
www.linkedin.com/feed/update/urn:li:activity:6418503725735
780352 (for Irena Politano)

7. **Bare your (professional) soul occasionally.** People like under-
standing who you are and what drives you. They like to know
you are *human*. Stay positive, but share a bit of your professional journey with us, as I've done here:
https://www.linkedin.com/posts/brendameller_sunday
inspiration-entrepreneur-enthusiasticallyunemployable-activ
ity-6571387825948815360-d85z

One final comment...
If every post from you is done using an automated service (Buffer, Meet
Edgar, etc.) and you never visit LinkedIn to check in on your network,
this isn't going to work. You need to be SOCIAL on LinkedIn and *engage*
with your connections. I personally LOVE Buffer, but it's a tool to help me
occasionally schedule postings on my business page; it's not a replacement for genuine engagement on my personal profile.

FYI my favorite pie is a good homemade sweet potato.
It's not in everyone's wheelhouse so I'm picky.
~ Tina Dews
www.linkedin.com/in/tmilldewsrecruiter

Section 6:

LinkedIn Company Page Strategy

Chapter 32:

LinkedIn Company Page Optimization

This Is A Pie Chart Describing My Favorite Bars.
And This Is A Bar Graph Describing My Favorite Pies.
~ Marshall Eriksen,
'How I Met Your Mother' TV Show

Once upon a time, in a land far, far away (circa 2006 and earlier), we marketers relied upon our website to be the point of destination for internet traffic.

Then, social media was born.

Nowadays, companies are harnessing the power of social media and establishing and maintaining their company presence on a variety of social and professional networking sites.

The great thing about social media is it provides businesses with an "opt-in" audience (for those who 'like' or follow your company page), as well as a way to attract potential future customers who may passively find a link to an article, update, blog, or other news linking them back to your LinkedIn company page.

WHY HAVE A LINKEDIN COMPANY PAGE?

LinkedIn company pages serve as an extension of your website. Websites are great, but only if you have visitors. By having a company page on LinkedIn, you may discover LinkedIn members who "stumble upon" your business and visit your company page.

When you have a LinkedIn company page and you've set up the page with your logo and linked your profile to your page, that annoying little gray building avatar goes away and it's replaced with your company logo.

Remember, GRAY IS NOT OK.

When I see a gray avatar next to someone's employer on their LinkedIn profile, it makes me think of a few things:

1. The company is no longer in business. This happens. It's part of business.

2. The person didn't correctly link to their employer page. This is where I swoop in wearing my superhero cape, offering pie and suggesting my services. Just kidding. But now I AM hungry for pie...

3. I wonder if the person *really* worked for that company, or if they are just making it up. Because if you work for a huge corporation, why wouldn't you have it linked on your profile. Unless you are lying about it. Are you lying? Did you REALLY work there?

4. The person never set up their company page. I see this as an opportunity that can quickly be fixed! Again, I swoop in and offer pie.

Do you have a LinkedIn company page? You should. The page is FREE and the requirements for creating a company page are simple.

Years ago, LinkedIn had several requirements to create a company page. Now, just about anybody with a LinkedIn profile can create a company page, as long as the page hasn't yet been created or claimed. I recommend you have a company page for your local non-profit organization, membership group, or professional networking chapter.

For example, here's a page for Detroit Together Digital (a local chapter of Together Digital): www.linkedin.com/company/detroit-together-digital

And also TEDxDetroit, a local affiliate of the TED organization: www.linkedin.com/company/tedxdetroit

HOW TO CREATE A COMPANY PAGE

1. In the upper right-hand corner in LinkedIn, click the little square with the nine dots that reads "Work."

2. Scroll down to the bottom of the options and then click, "Create a Company Page."

3. Follow the instructions to set up your page.

Don't worry about the page being 100% perfect when you set it up. You can change just about every field after it's set up, and some fields you can leave blank for now.

"Great Brenda. I have my page. But you said you were going to help me OPTIMIZE my page. How do I do THAT? It sounds magical and fabulous."

It is and you're right!

Here's how to optimize your LinkedIn company page:

1. **Fill out every area and use all your character limits.** Just like with your profile, look at your company page in both collapsed view and in full view, in desktop view and in mobile view. Make sure what you're adding on your company page looks good in *all* views.

2. **Logo: include your current logo, and consider an abbreviated version or favicon version of the logo.** It's going to be tiny, so might as well make it the biggest small image you can, if you know what I mean. Sometimes you may see company pages that have an animated logo. This was a feature that LinkedIn used to offer page admins, but it's no longer an option. Those of us who uploaded a gif can keep it in, but if I ever want to change my logo, I lose my animated gif privileges.

3. **Page header: create an image that helps to sell your business.** Think about this the same way you think about billboards on the side of the highway. Use this space for a branded image, a key message, promoting a product, service, or event, celebrating an achievement, or giving people a glimpse into your culture. And, just like a billboard, change this periodically. Ideally, once per quarter, but you could change it more frequently. Consider using an image that mirrors your website. Your goal here is brand consistency.

4. **Add a tagline.** You have 120 characters to tell us your story. Speak to your ideal target audience, just like in your personal profile.

5. **Fill out your overview about your company.** You have 2,000 characters to tell us your company story. Include:
   a. A few sentences describing your company at a high-level. Mirror what you have on your website.

   b. A list of your products and services. You want to do business on LinkedIn, don't you? Then let's not make it difficult for people to know what you are selling. At this point, if they have landed on your company page and they are reading, you have drawn them in. Kudos, by the way. Nice work!

   c. A contact email, phone number, or web page. Make it EASY for people to do business with you. Don't make them hunt around for a contact section. Even if it's RIGHT THERE under "website" – just assume they don't see it and put the website in there again. It's not clickable within this block, but they could easily copy / paste or just type it in.

6. **Start posting on your company page.** For your first post, I suggest this:

   "Welcome to the official LinkedIn company for [company name]. Please FOLLOW our page for LinkedIn strategy tips and to learn about our upcoming events."

7. **Make sure your employees all link your company page to their individual profiles.** If your logo appears, they are all set. If not, have them go into their EXPERIENCE section to edit the company name until the logo appears.

8. **Keep posting on your company page.** Ideally, I recommend you post at minimum once a month, but ideally 2-3x/week.

9. **Monitor your page for likes (reactions), comments, and shares.** Assign someone to invite new page followers / post likes to connect. Assign someone to reply to all comments with responses of at least five words. Assign someone to reply to all shared posts to thank people for sharing with a 5+ word response.

NOTE: As you're building your page, have it open in a second tab and click "VIEW AS MEMBER" so you can see the fields as you are building the page.

I could seriously write a whole other book on LinkedIn company pages. They serve as such amazing business tools. Stay tuned, and when you're reading this chapter, check out the Meller Marketing company page on LinkedIn *www.linkedin.com/company/meller-marketing-llc* and comment on my latest post to ask me how my next book on LinkedIn company pages is coming along.

While you're there, check out my other LinkedIn company page strategy tips.

My favorite pie is apple. Cherry is my second favorite.
~ Lori Knudsen
www.linkedin.com/in/lori-knudsen

Chapter 33:

How to Grow Your LinkedIn Company Page Followers

Dorothy: Oh, Ma, I'm making dinner.
What would you like to eat?
Sophia: A nice, thick T-bone steak, corn on the cob,
and pecan pie for dessert. Now ask me what I can chew!
~ Scene from 'Golden Girls'

There are three keys to success to help grow your company page views:

1. **People need to know about the page.**

2. **You need to post interesting content to the page.**

3. **Your content needs to prompt your page followers to engage with your page content (like, comment, share).**

Let's break each down.

1. PEOPLE NEED TO KNOW ABOUT YOUR PAGE

If a tree falls in a forest and nobody is around, does it make a sound? The same concept applies for your company page. If it exists and nobody knows about it, how can they follow it?

Here are several tips to help promote your company page:

➤ Post on your personal profile and announce that you have launched a company page for your business on LinkedIn. Tag your company page in the post. Ask people to give your page a follow.

➤ Add your LinkedIn company page link on your company's website. Make sure you have the link set to "open in a new page" so they don't navigate completely off your website.

➤ Post on other social networks to invite people to follow your company page on LinkedIn, and include the link to your company page.

➤ Message connections who are in your inner circle and send them a personal request to follow your company page. Include the link to make it easy for them. If it feels weird to message them, they are not in your inner circle. Consider your cheerleaders and top promoters, close friends, and family members.

➤ Make sure you have added/linked your company page to your EXPERIENCE section of your profile and that the logo is clickable to your company page:

➤ Ask your employees to make sure they have linked your employer on their profile. NOTE: Employees automatically "FOLLOW" a company page.

Self-employed? Independent consultant? You should have a company page, too. Having a company page on LinkedIn is a way to generate more leads for your business, and is the equivalent of using a company email instead of a Gmail; it shows you are serious and a well-established business.

2. YOU NEED TO POST INTERESTING CONTENT TO YOUR COMPANY PAGE

Once you have created your page, you need to start adding content to it. Do this in the form of posts on the page.

➤ **Post regularly and frequently.** I recommend you post 2-3 times per week on your company page. Include a blend of selling and telling. Selling = promoting your products and services. Telling = sharing photos of you and your employees. Share experiences of working with clients or network connections. Telling = any post that DOES NOT SELL. Make sure you have a blend of both. I would err on the side of two posts of "TELLING" content to one post of "SELLING" content. The goal here is to be interesting. Selling is not interesting. Sorry!

I read a LinkedIn blog[19] that recommended a 3-2-1 approach in your company page postings. For every six posts:

> ❯ 3 should be sharing industry articles
> ❯ 2 should be posts that make your employees feel proud about the company
> ❯ 1 should be selling your company

➤ **Give them free samples.** People LOVE getting stuff for free. It's like when I go to Grand Traverse Pie in Troy, Michigan. They offer free pie samples (I kid you not). I always try the samples. *And guess what?* Sometimes I end up buying another slice of the pie I've sampled to take home and share with my family. You can do the same on your company page on LinkedIn. Periodically share advice. Give them a quick tip or two.

---

19   business.linkedin.com/marketing-solutions/blog/linkedin-company-pages/
2019/the-ultimate-guide-to-improve-your-b2b-content-marketing-strateg

➤ **Share content from other people and other sources.** There are many ways to find content to post on your company page, including:

   ❭ I use Feedly.com to source content.

   ❭ When you're reading an article from a magazine website, from another place on social media, or in doing research for a client or project, imagine me tapping you on the shoulder saying, "HEY LYNN: YOU SHOULD SHARE THAT ON YOUR COMPANY PAGE."

   ❭ Look at LinkedIn's content suggestions.

> When you post the link, **add a comment of five or more words** telling people what it is about or something you've learned from reading the article. This helps to demonstrate your expertise.

➤ **Look at what your TOP aspirational competitors are posting.** You will get inspiration on what works well in a company page post. Pay attention to posts that generate a lot of engagement (likes and comments) vs. those that generate only one like or zero likes.

3. YOUR CONTENT NEEDS TO PROMPT YOUR PAGE FOLLOWERS TO ENGAGE WITH YOUR PAGE CONTENT (LIKE, COMMENT, SHARE)

➤ **Include a call-to-action in some (but not all) of your posts.** Encourage people to "comment below to add your thoughts" or ask open-ended questions like, "What do you think?"

➤ **When considering a post, ask yourself:** *would I like this?* Would I comment on this? Would I share this? If not, you need to get more shareable content.

➤ **Periodically (once a week), share a post from your company page to your personal LinkedIn network.** You will need to change from "admin" to "view as member" to see the SHARE icon. Yes, it's perfectly OK to do this. I do this. And while you're at it, make sure you add a comment of five or more words, plus a suggestion that "if you found this interesting, please follow my company page here on LinkedIn."

➤ **Encourage your employees to SHARE posts from your company page** and make sure you are thanking them on that post when they share. There's even a new feature on LinkedIn in 2020 which enables a page admin to broadcast page posts out to ALL employees, notifying them of new page posts. Do this sparingly; maybe once a week. I'd also recommend an email sent from you to all employees alerting them of this feature and asking for their help in engaging with your company page content. Yes! It's OK to do so!

➤ **Encourage your employees to LIKE and COMMENT (with five or more words)** on your company page posts. When they do so, acknowledge them. Thank them for comments by replying back with a comment from the company page. Yes, it's OK to do this. It provides positive reinforcement for your employees.

➤ **Make it social.** When someone comments on a company page post, respond back. Even if they say, "great article" or something similar, reply back with five or more words. Example, "Thank you for your comment, Chris. Have a great weekend!" Do this even if it's an employee. In fact, ESPECIALLY if it's an employee!

In 2020, LinkedIn also gave all pages the ability to invite connections to follow your company page. As of the time this book was written, you could send out 100 invites to follow from within the company page, and you have to be a page admin to use this feature.

I send out all 100 invites, and as the invites are accepted, LinkedIn issues me invite "credits" back to invite more followers. I max these out every month, and look forward to the first day of the month when I can send out another batch of 100 new page follow invitations.

In addition, I've recently started requesting my new connections to follow my LinkedIn company page for more LinkedIn strategy tips. *The results?* I've grown my page followers by a little over 1,000 in just a month.

I love pie too but not the coffee. Gotta be tea for me!
~ Jessica Jones
www.linkedin.com/in/askjessicajones

Section 7:

Miscellaneous & Conclusion

Chapter 34:

LinkedIn Errors & Hiccups

Dr. Cristina Yang: Yea hi, did you bring liquor?
Joe: No, I brought pie. Pumpkin.
Dr. Cristina Yang: You're a bartender how did you not
bring liquor?
Joe: Did you bring scalpels?
~ Scene from 'Grey's Anatomy' TV show

There's one consistent thing about LinkedIn that I know I can rely on after years of being active on this platform, coaching executives and teams, and sharing insights with fellow LinkedIn trainers and coaches, and that's this: LinkedIn can be wonky.

No, that's not their "official" word but it's the best way to explain the fact that sometimes, you will experience odd hiccups and glitches on LinkedIn that have no explanation.

This is why I always advise clients to do profile creation offline in a Word document or some other electronic place that can save as you go.

If you spend an hour working on your LinkedIn headline and then go to save, it will (I promise you) give you a weird error message about saving here or refreshing this page, and you'll hit the button that seems to be the right one and – VOILA! – everything you just worked on is *gone.*

Yes, I know this for a fact because this has happened to me, too.

Sometimes, I get lucky and it's during a client session that I'm delivering via Zoom and we can watch the recording to capture the missing text on screen before it went missing.

But, most of the time, all your hard work is gone.

Gone, like a homemade slice of pie that fell off your plate as you were carrying it from the counter to the table and, of course, it lands facedown. Well, in this case at least you have the memories of the pie to look at, but if your work disappears on LinkedIn, you become frantic and you're in denial that it's really gone.

Yes, gone forever. The quicker you realize and learn from this, the better off you'll be.

WHY – OH WHY – IS LINKEDIN SO GLITCHY?

Here's my theory. Consider the fact that LinkedIn never has any scheduled downtime. It's always up. My hypothesis is that when you're experiencing a glitch on LinkedIn, it's because LinkedIn is in the middle of launching updates and you got stuck in the site at the time they refreshed the site to roll out all the changes.

Sometimes, it's not just new profile content. At times, it might be tags or mentions that were once there and suddenly go missing (or become untagged). Or, you may post on your company page and it's there, but then it's not there.

> NOTE: If this happens and you're the company page admin, give it a minute. Don't repost (yes, I've done this).

Chances are, it will magically appear on the company page in about a minute or two. Hit refresh a few times. Sip your coffee. Go get a new slice of pie.

Get me a slice too, while you're up. All this talk about pie is making me hungry!

Ok, refresh again. Now it's there.

And if you didn't listen to me earlier and you posted it AGAIN, you'll see two posts there (yes, this has happened to me).

If you have a super active community, you may have already generated a few likes and a comment or two on BOTH posts, and now you have to make a decision about which of the duplicate posts to delete (yes, this has happened to me. Aren't you glad you are learning from my experience?).

This reminds me of ketchup stuck in the bottle. You dump the bottle over. You can see it coming out slowly, so you hit the bottle a bit and then BAM you've got more ketchup than any French fry should ever see in a serving. If you had only waited and had some patience, you would have served yourself a perfect dollop.

Sometimes, you try to do something and it's worked 100 times before, and now it won't work at all.

It could be updating your ABOUT paragraph. Reorganizing your skills list. Approving a recommendation. Whatever it is, it's not working.

No, this is not you. It's LinkedIn being glitchy.

If refreshing your page doesn't fix the issue, do what I do. Open up another internet browser. If you're usually using Chrome, try Internet Explorer or Firefox. Do the thing you wanted to do. Save.

Most often, this fixes the glitch. You're welcome.

If not, you should probably take a LinkedIn break and come back later.

Sometimes, the issue won't resolve itself for a few hours and then when you go back to LinkedIn, there may be some new navigation areas or features that weren't there before.

I like to use this analogy. If you have pets and live near an area that has an earthquake, you may see your dog or cat running through the house just a few seconds before the earthquake begins. You have no idea how or why they know something weird is coming, but they just know.

Same with LinkedIn: if it's glitchy, it's probably because they are rolling out some changes.

To summarize:

➤ Glitches are common on LinkedIn. It's not just you.
➤ If you don't want to lose any new profile edits, create them elsewhere and then copy/paste them in when you're done working on the edit.
➤ Be really careful when carrying pie from the counter to the table.
➤ If you post on your company page and can't find what you posted, wait a few minutes before posting again. It's probably there and it's just not visible yet. Be patient, because it's like ketchup coming out of the bottle.
➤ Anyone else hungry for pie? No? Just me?

My favorite pie is pecan pie.
~ Areej Mustafa
www.linkedin.com/in/areejmustafa

Chapter 35:

Stealth Mode

*You know what they say: 'Why sit at a table that doesn't
have key lime pie on it if you don't have to?'*
                                                    ~ Sloane Crosley

Don't worry, I won't tell your boss you flipped to this chapter to read it *first*.

Ever notice how some people seem to really "get" LinkedIn, and their career transitions seem effortless as a result? Thinking about using LinkedIn for your next career change, but don't want your employer to know? Here are a few LinkedIn strategy tips for those of you seeking to use LinkedIn and you need to go into "stealth mode."

This is just my fancy way of packaging up the tips in this chapter. There's not a "stealth mode" button anywhere on your profile. That WOULD be pretty cool though, right?!?

FIRST: Let's talk about your connections.
Consider your connections and who you really want to stay connected with at your current organization. If you're still working at the company, it may be poor form to disconnect from your boss and coworkers. However, your boss might not be active on LinkedIn nor even notice it.

Back in 2008, when I was using LinkedIn to make a job change, I disconnected from the president of my company along with my boss. Neither were active on LinkedIn, and neither would be individuals I would continue to keep in contact with after I left the company.

When you disconnect, they don't get a notification. They just simply no longer see your posts in their homepage feed (unless a lot of people they are connected to are engaging with your posts). And, if they visit your profile, they would see they are now a second-level connection.

This helps to reduce the visibility for people seeing your LinkedIn activity. In my case, there was little-to-no risk.

If you're worried they may notice or disconnecting may set off red flags, don't do it. But I would visit their profiles and hit "unfollow" if you no longer wish to see their updates.

NEXT: Let's increase your focus on your company on your profile.

Look at all of your LinkedIn activities as a way to demonstrate that you are a positive brand ambassador for your company.

"Wait… WHAT?," you're thinking– right?

Yes, follow along with me on this.

You can do this by:

> ➤ Making sure your employer is linked on your profile, that you have a one- or two-sentence description of your employer, a few sentences describing your company's products and services, and no more than one sentence about your role in your experience section. You can include your specialties in a keyword list, but

make sure your experience doesn't read the same as your resume. This is NOT a resume and not a time to be looking like you've copied / pasted your resume into your profile. That's a red flag!

➤ Liking, commenting, and sharing your company page updates at least once a week.

➤ Reviewing your contact info to make sure your company website is listed as one of the three web pages. You will have to give some thought to whether to keep your employer email as your primary email or change it to your home email. By changing it, you might alert people that you're considering making a move. Therefore, you may be better off leaving it as your work email and, if you happen to receive any inquiries to your work email, go onto LinkedIn and reply to them from there instead.

➤ Using your header image to support your company and its brand. Look like the best brand ambassador out there and nobody will suspect a thing. Make sure your headshot photo is current and the best professional representation of you as well.

➤ Liking and commenting on your coworkers' posts, especially those in leadership positions or those who are super active on LinkedIn. Again, this is a strategy to throw people off the chase, because a person interacting with their coworkers on LinkedIn looks like a great online networker who is a huge brand and company supporter. Personally, I'd recommend you focus on people with large networks or those who may be connected to people or organizations you're targeting in your job search.

First, think about this from the perspective of your coworkers. They see you stepping up your LinkedIn activity, and it makes you look like you are more (*not less*) engaged with the company. You are building brand visibility for your company– and thereby for yourself.

Second, think about this from the perspective of hiring managers and people who could refer you to new positions. They see your activity, and the fact that you are a rockstar for your company. If you were a hiring manager, would you rather have somebody who is a positive brand ambassador (as can be seen by their current LinkedIn activity), or someone who is neutral or who seems desperate?

I'd rather look at the rockstar and try to lure them away because if they are rocking for my competitor, they will rock for me too.

ALSO: Don't be obvious!

Stop throwing off all those red flags. The first thing I notice for someone who is considering a job search is a flurry of new recommendations given to them in a short amount of time.

What I recommend to my clients is you are *always* giving and requesting recommendations, whether you're job searching or not. If you haven't had any recommendations in years, focus on giving a few in the next few months, and requesting a new recommendation every other month. Spread them out so it's not so obvious and focus on GIVING recommendations.

In addition, by no means should you ever post your resume as a PDF *anywhere* on your public LinkedIn profile if you're using the platform to find a new job while working. That's like leaving your resume on the copy machine at work. AWKWARD.

SOME OTHER REMINDERS...

LinkedIn is NOT a job search website, it's a professional networking site.

Read that last sentence out loud. Now read it again. And read it one more time if you still don't believe me. Even if your conscious mind doesn't accept it yet, your subconscious will start to believe it and make it true. That's the same reason why I write affirmations on my white board and read them every day. My mind will find a way to make it happen if I believe it.

Many clients I work with approach me because they are not at all active on LinkedIn and now they find themselves in a situation where they need to use LinkedIn for a job search and they don't know where to begin. They are also hesitant to get active on LinkedIn because they don't want their employer thinking they are job searching.

Change your perspective, and the way that you USE LinkedIn will change, too. LinkedIn is NOT a job search website. It's a professional networking site that has some job search features. However, it's used more by working professionals who are NOT job seeking than it is used by job seekers.

Yes, there is a job search board– but not everybody uses is.

Yes, recruiters are searching profiles on LinkedIn, but it doesn't mean YOUR profile will come up in their searches, even if you are qualified for the job and an ideal candidate.

Simply having a profile and being active on LinkedIn doesn't mean you are job searching. If it did, then that would mean that there are 722 million+ people who are on LinkedIn looking for jobs. That's just not likely.

Are you convinced that LinkedIn is not a job search site yet? Because it's not. Really. I wouldn't lie to you. I want you to trust me.

LinkedIn is a professional networking site and I'm just glad that you're thinking about making a job move AND you're open to getting more active on LinkedIn AND that you're reading this book! I'm looking out for you and I want to help.

But if I do help you, I want you to promise me that you'll get active on LinkedIn and STAY ACTIVE – long after you've landed your next dream job.

The best way to get started is to go slowly. This will help YOU and will also help you to build up your comfort level and confidence in that what I'm telling you is all true.

So, let's go slow. Here's what you're going to do:

1. **Connect with me if we're not yet connected.** I'll sprinkle LinkedIn tips into my timeline every day just for you. By connecting with me, my posts will start appearing in your homepage feed like magic.

2. **Every business day, spend 15 minutes in your LinkedIn homepage feed.** The first week or so, you'll just be reading. Reading posts, reading comments, reading articles.

    Reading is perfectly OK. Before we run, we have to learn how to crawl, right? This exercise will help you to get comfortable with how people are using LinkedIn. You'll start to notice what resonates with you and what doesn't. You'll start to notice posts that do really well and get a lot of likes and comments, and those that get a like or two and that's it. Or, those that don't get any likes at all. Keep doing this until you're ready to move on.

    Are you ready for the next step? This is going to involve action on your part, and it's going to increase your visibility. Both are good things.

3. **Every business day, scroll through your homepage feed and add a like to 2-3 posts.** You can pick any 2-3 posts you want. Keep scrolling until you find them. Now, if this were me, I'd focus on posts that are getting a lot of engagement already, or posts made by people who can be resources to me during my job search. I like to build social media karma with people who can help me.

4. **Then, pick one of those posts to add a comment onto, using five or more words for your comment.** It doesn't need to be anything too intellectual. Just pretend you're standing right next to the person and they read their post out loud. What would you say back to them? That's your comment. Don't overthink this. (You're overthinking this right now aren't you? JUST STOP.)

I guarantee if you do these steps in order, you're going to start to see a few things happen on your LinkedIn.

First, your profile views will increase. That's pretty exciting to see that trend line start increasing. It will spike. Just ask Matt Dibble (www.linkedin.com/in/matthewdibble).

www.linkedin.com/posts/matthewdibble_brenda-meller-straight-changing-the-game-activity-6594608395339259904-UcKh

Second, you will start to get more invitations to connect. Being active on LinkedIn will jumpstart inbound invitations. Keep in mind that one of these new connections might be a referral to your next dream job, so don't be quite as picky as you used to be about accepting connections. You never know!

Third, you will gain more confidence about how other people are using LinkedIn. You'll start to become aware of the fact that LinkedIn is not a job search site, it's a professional networking site. Wait… where have you heard this before? Sounds so familiar…

Fourth, you might get an inkling to post yourself on LinkedIn. If so, my work here is done and it's time to give me a review on Amazon and tell someone else to buy my book.

But seriously, posting on LinkedIn is a good thing. All that work that you've put into reading and responding to others posts was like a training ground for you. (Anyone remember Karate Kid? Wax on, wax off…)

Now, you're ready to start posting.

5. **Once a week, post on LinkedIn.** If you've been following my instructions in order, this step should seem natural and comfortable.

If you're still concerned that LinkedIn is a job search site, go back to step one. And this time, really read the steps and follow the actions I recommend. Don't just skim. (Aha! Caught you, didn't I?!?)

By reading and observing from others, you should have a good sense of what works and what doesn't work. You're not posting to tell your network that you're searching for a new position. Instead, you're posting to share insights, observations, inspiration, articles, news, or other information that others might find interesting. The goal here is to simply start posting so you can increase visibility for yourself.

Hopefully these tips have made you feel like you've earned a highly coveted "stealth mode" badge on LinkedIn, and these strategies help you to find that next dream job.

As a side note, I am a big believer in positive thinking, and if you envision yourself landing your next dream job, I believe your mind WILL find a way to make it happen. You have to open your heart and mind to the possibilities and the potential in your everyday life.

It's like buying a used car. You never notice them until one day when you start to think about buying another car because your current car needs more repairs and is giving you concern. Then suddenly, you start to see used cars in parking lots. You see cars with "for sale" signs while stopped in traffic. You start to notice Facebook ads for cars, and you start to hear conversations about people who are considering selling their cars.

Once your mind is open to an idea, you will start to notice what has been there all along.

The same is true with LinkedIn. You can leverage LinkedIn as a job search tool while working and minimize the visibility of your job search while maximizing YOUR visibility as a LinkedIn user.

When you hear from connections, "Wow MiVida, I'm seeing your LinkedIn posts every day. You post amazing nonprofit tips," then you know it's working.

When someone from your marketing or sales team compliments you on your LinkedIn activity at the beginning of your work meeting, you know it's working. Especially when they suggest to other employees to look at your profile as an example of a LinkedIn 'super user.' (And you can totally take all the credit for this. You don't even need to tell them it was my idea.)

Just like Dorothy in her ruby red slippers, the power was there all along. You just need to believe it and take control.

Did Auntie Em bake pie in the Wizard of Oz movie? I'm sure she did and it was apple or cherry or something delicious.

Olalliberry Pie. Hands down my favorite pie. That's all I wanted for my birthday growing up and I loved it every time. (Yes, I still have it for my birthday each year).
~ Adam McKee Miller
www.linkedin.com/in/mckeemiller

Chapter 36:

LinkedIn Live

*Martin: I have something that'll cheer you up. I brought
you some of Sherry's mock apple pie. It's called "mock"
cause they uses crackers instead of apples.
Frasier: Good. Nothing spoils an apple pie like apples.*
~ from 'Frasier' TV show

As of the time I'm writing this, LinkedIn LIVE video is still S-L-O-W-L-Y rolling out across the network. Also at this time, there is an application process, and the insiders at LinkedIn are being very selective on who gets access.

I was finally granted access on November 18, 2019 after applying *three* times. *Three.* I know what you're thinking– don't they know who I am?

All kidding aside, I was ELATED when I realized I had been given access. The first I knew of this discovery was when I noticed the red dot and LinkedIn LIVE in my left navigation on the home page. (Note: this no longer shows on your profile.)

It reads:

LinkedIn Live.

Your profile has access to broadcast live video on LinkedIn. Get started now.

The "get started now" was a link which led me to this page:

www.linkedin.com/help/linkedin/answer/100225

The page basically explains that you have to choose a live streaming provider to start streaming live video on LinkedIn.

I evaluated all of the options by clicking the links and going to their home-pages. I immediately eliminated the services where I couldn't find pricing on their homepage or through a link. My thought here is that if they aren't making it easy to find a price on what is a commoditized service, their customer service and/or marketing is probably not that good either.

I then focused on the options that were lower priced, as I am in the test-ing phase of this new offering, and I don't want to spend thousands of dollars a year on this.

Plus, the equipment I'm using is simple: a desktop webcam, sometimes a microphone, sometimes earphones, office lighting, and a home Wi-Fi connection via my laptop. I wanted a solution that would work with what I had and didn't cost too much.

I also focused on solutions which offered a free trial.

I selected StreamYard. Then, I did what any parent of a tech-expert teen would do: I asked my son to look at all the options to see if he agreed. He did.

Of course, I checked with him to make sure he actually read through the list and looked at the spec requirements. Keep in mind that my son has been super active online in the gaming and YouTube community for years. He also has experience live streaming on YouTube and using video equipment, so I knew he'd be honest with me.

I then signed up for a free account on StreamYard and followed the links to add my accounts. I added my LinkedIn profile and then followed the instructions to start a broadcast live on LinkedIn. I added a brief video title and clicked.

Then, it took me a few minutes to figure out how to share my screen so I could show people my LinkedIn view. And after a minute of live streaming and talking, I realized the audio and video weren't displaying, so I adjusted those settings and tried again.

At this point, I picked up my phone. I've learned one thing over the years of doing live broadcasts via webinars and Facebook: check out your audio/video to make sure people can see and hear you.

On my phone, a notification popped up that I was LIVE on LinkedIn. I clicked the link on my phone and it took me to the feed where the video was showing. There is a slight delay, I'm guessing 20-30 seconds, and I was able to see comments people were leaving for me.

I've seen other people delivering LinkedIn live who have a moderator for their comments. I've also seen some people wait to reply to the comments later so they could focus on their messages in the live video.

Me? I was just testing this whole process out and making mistakes along the way, and telling people who were watching me live about the mistakes and what I've learned and how not to make the same mistakes.

I think the highest I reached while in Live video was 118 viewers, but I'm not able to confirm. You can see the playback at this link:

www.linkedin.com/video/live/urn:li:activity:660265015725
7408513/

MY ADVICE FOR YOU REGARDING LINKEDIN LIVE

1. **Want access? Be patient.** As of today, you have to apply to get access to LinkedIn Live. I applied three times to get access. The first time, I received an automated email from LinkedIn saying, "thanks for your application but no" or something to that effect.

    Then I started asking around to all the cool people I know who had LinkedIn live. Sometimes I would join them in THEIR live sessions to ask questions about their streaming software.

2. **Get comfortable with the uncomfortable.** If you really want LinkedIn Live access, get practice on webinars or Facebook Live (Which requires NO application process. Just click "LIVE" and go!). The more practice you have with thinking on your feet, the more comfortable you'll be when you finally do get access.

    In my first video, I made a few mistakes. That's OK. I'm still a good person. Plus, I turned those mistakes into learning opportunities to share with my viewing community. Guess what? They loved it! I received a handful of messages afterward from people saying they appreciated my genuine nature and showing them behind the scenes. It was like sharing PIE with the whole family!

    I indicated to my community several times throughout the video that this was my first LIVE broadcast. I try to never apologize for my mistakes, but rather tell people what I did wrong and how to prevent the mistake. I also thanked people at the end for watching and being a part of my "inaugural" LinkedIn live video, and mentioned that someday we would all look back together at how far we've come.

3. **Jump on as many LIVE videos as you can.** I did this in the month leading up to the time I was approved. When I joined, I would leave a comment "hello from Metro Detroit" or something similar. My name was mentioned by many of those live hosts during their session, and I even got a few shout-outs.

4. **Be a guest on as many LIVE videos as you can**. Before I was given LinkedIn live access, I was a LinkedIn Live guest a few times. By going through this experience, I learned many things. One of which is that when you close off a live broadcast, after you sign off, keep the screen up for a few seconds so you aren't cutting your conversation off before the live stream ends.

5. **Have good equipment.** Make the best of what you have, and know when it's time to invest in better equipment. Read this: www.mellermarketing.com/post/hey-brenda-what-tech-do-you-use

6. **Stage your backdrop.** Before you start live streaming, look at your screen and notice what is behind you in the camera's view. Move your desk to another area if needed or move items that appear behind you. Before my first video, I moved my desk chair so my viewers would not see the wall outlet on my white wall.

7. **Repurpose your video content.** After my first broadcast ended, I immediately went into StreamYard and downloaded the video, then uploaded it to my Camtasia video editing software and clipped out the first minute of black screen. Then, I created a cover graphic, added it to the video, and created an MP4 version that I saved on my laptop. Then, I uploaded it to YouTube. You can watch the video here: youtu.be/L_HxtyEyMmI

From there, you can also upload the video to Facebook or share the link on Twitter. Create content once, and merchandise in multiple places.

You can also show the live link in your FEATURED section.

8. **Watch your comments.** Part of the appeal of LinkedIn live is the live, near real-time interaction. It reminds me of events broadcast on live TV when you try to get in the background, and you're so excited when people say they saw you on TV.

The same goes for LinkedIn: people like to be a part of the LIVE action. Keep in mind that there are 2-3 potential participants in your live video:
> 1 – You
> 2 – Your interviewee (if you are interviewing someone)
> 3 – Your live viewers (including your community)

My perspective is that if you ignore your community and your viewers and you aren't a national celebrity, major organization, or some other notable figure of leader in industry, people aren't going to watch you.

You have to *engage* with your community. Part of the reason my first live video was such a success is that I mentioned everyone by name and read their comments and questions to everyone. I made them feel special because they made ME feel special! GROUP HUG EVERYONE.

During the video, I recommend you look for live comments only after the stream has been up for a few minutes. This allows you to keep the focus first on you and the live broadcast, and also allows time for people to make their comments and for those comments to show up in your feed with the delay.

After the session ends, monitor your comments for the next day or so, as your video will continue to gain viewers even after the live broadcast ends. Easy as pie, right?

My favorite pie is chocolate pecan...what's yours?
~ Pat Altvater
www.linkedin.com/in/pataltvater

Chapter 37:

How to ROCK on LinkedIn in Just 15 Minutes a Day

*A friend like a piece of pie: You can never have too many
and they make you happy when you're sad.*

~ Unknown

"**B**renda, you look like you're on LinkedIn ALL THE TIME. I don't have that much time to spend. How much time do I need to spend on LinkedIn each week?"

This is a common statement and question I hear.

First of all, I'm not on LinkedIn all the time. I just spend my time very strategically during every visit.

I'm a big believer in social media karma, and I've also learned that every post, every like, every company post, and any other action I take on LinkedIn should be intentional. I am always thinking of my target audience, and why they care about this post or action, and how it helps ME to reach business goals.

Want to rock on LinkedIn? Here's my advice for you.

Think about LinkedIn the same way you think about your work email: it's a communication channel. How many days would you go without checking your work email? Probably not even one day. You have learned the importance of communication through email and you check it every day, and perhaps even several times a day. But you have also learned that if you keep your email open, your day quickly slips away from you and you aren't productive with the items you needed to do that day.

I recommend you spend 15 minutes a day on LinkedIn, every single business day. There's no magic to spending 15 instead of 10 or 20 minutes, but I have found that if you can commit 15 minutes a day on LinkedIn every single business day, you WILL see an improvement in your results.

Part of this is just changing behavior and getting you into the habit of being more active on LinkedIn every day.

Part of this is spending enough time on LinkedIn every day to do something worthwhile.

Here are a few techniques I've learned about how to best spend those 15 minutes. I invite you to add other techniques to this list, and then rotate through the list until you find out what works best for you.

1. **Focus on your homepage feed.** Spend a few minutes during every LinkedIn visit on your homepage. Read through posts. Like those that resonate with you. Comment on those where it makes sense to comment. Treat this like you would reading the newspaper, or scanning your inbox.

2. **Go through business cards you've collected and invite people to connect.** Chances are, you have a binder, or drawer, or a bowl of business cards (or, if you're like me, a pie tin full of business cards) you've collected over the years. Look those people up on LinkedIn and send a personalized invitation to connect if

you're not connected yet. Already connected? Awesome. Now go and add a comment to one of their latest posts.

3. **Review your invitations.** Don't ignore invites from those you don't know. Instead, look at their profiles. (That way, they'll see that you've looked at their profile.) Then, reply with, "Hi [first name], thanks for the invite. Have we met?" This acknowledgment starts a conversation that can help you to determine if this connection could be mutually beneficial.

4. **Pick a group on LinkedIn to engage with each week.** Start by responding to posts made within the group with likes or comments. Then, post something in the group. Respond to others in the group. Send invitations to other group members. Repeat again next week with a different group.

5. **Research your competition.** If you're seeking a way to enhance your profile on LinkedIn, try this simple technique, which will help to educate you as well as offer you insights on the competition. Type in your job title in the search box, then click on "PEOPLE" to look at people only. If you're looking to extend beyond those you know, then filter the list to include 2nd or 3rd+ level connections.

6. **Review and update your profile.** It's important to keep in mind that your LinkedIn profile should be reviewed periodically, just as you should do with your resume. Why? Your career changes. You gain new responsibilities. Your accomplishments change. You may add new volunteer activities, too. Read your About statement. Does it inspire you or bore you to tears? If it's the latter, change it now. *Today.* Look for other people on LinkedIn with similar job titles if you need inspiration. Or look at mine!

7. **Cruise your contacts.** Being a good networker means staying active with your LinkedIn connections. It's easy to become so

focused on growing your connections list that you might forget the value of each connection gained along the way. And you don't usually make time to reach out to your connections until you need something. (It's okay, it happens to me, too!) Pick a few people from your connections list and send them a greeting to check-in (without soliciting business). Something like, *"Hi Mark, it's been almost a decade since we worked together at PMH. Can you believe it? Hope you and the family are well. Brenda Meller"*

OR, something like this:
> Start off where you last left off with this person: "When we last chatted, you were working on…[insert activity here] and I'm curious how things are going."
> Include an update of where you're working now and a one-line description of the company and your role.
> DON'T solicit. Especially if it's the first time you've reached out in a long time.
> End with an offer: "If there's ever anything you need, let me know."

8. **Review / update (or share a post from) your company page.** If you have a company page on LinkedIn, make sure you review the page content every few months. Your services may change. Your description may need to be modified. Or, you might wish to change your background header image to something new and exciting.

If you're an employee of a company and notice something incorrect or outdated on your company page, let your marketing department know. They will appreciate that you're looking out for them!

You could also spend a few minutes reviewing your company page posts and taking a few minutes to select one to share as a post. Make sure you add at least five words when you share.

9. **Export your connections list.** This is something I will do once or twice a year. The benefit of exporting your connections list is that it exports into a csv format which you can easily convert into Excel to sort and review your connections. The export list no longer contains email addresses (unless the person specifically gives permission to include it in exports – which people rarely do), but you can review the list and then go back into LinkedIn to find their email on their account in their contact info section. Just please do not add people to your email list unless they have given permission. Not only is it rude to do so, but you also violate CAN-SPAM laws by doing so.

10. **Screen invitations.** The longer you're on LinkedIn and the more active you become, you'll notice you receive more and more invitations to connect to people you don't know. Spend a few minutes once a week replying with a message to these unknown invitations.

11. **Give your connections endorsements for their skills.** Scan through people in your connections list and visit their profiles, then give them endorsements for a few skills that you know are at their core area of expertise. Not only are you building social media karma, but they will also get a notification of your endorsement, which may build dialog.

12. **Check out your competitors' pages.** This is not stalking, this is research. Let them inspire you. Leave a comment if you're feeling bold. I do! But I see all of my competitors as "coopetition."

13. **Give someone in your network a recommendation.** Think about someone you have recently done business with, worked with, or served on a committee or nonprofit board or professional group with, where you can speak to their expertise. It's well worth the 15 minutes it takes to give them the recommendation for the social media karma it creates.

14. **Post a LinkedIn blog using the "Write an article on LinkedIn" feature.** It may take you more than 15 minutes, but you can start the process with an outline, then work on writing a bit each day until you're ready to post it.

15. **Post and ask people a general question, such as, "What advice would you offer to a college graduate just getting started on LinkedIn?"** Then, comment with a response to each one. Here are the responses from when I posted this a few years ago:

"Customize the URL."
~ Christopher G. Johnson, MBA,
www.linkedin.com/in/cgjohnson/

"Get a professional picture taken."
~ Laura Rolands,
www.linkedin.com/in/laurarolands/

"It's not about how many contacts you have but the quality of contacts!"
~ Kara (Bundenthal) Caruth, MSF, CFP®,
www.linkedin.com/in/karacaruth/

"Join groups and comment in them. Whenever I post in a group I get people looking at my profile."
~ Trish Belanger, CPA, MST
www.linkedin.com/in/trishb1040

"Be sure to add keywords to your profile. And avoid a selfie for your profile pic! Also, they should be adding projects to showcase their abilities."
~ Erin Janda Rawlings,
www.linkedin.com/in/erinjandarawlings/

"Ask their profs if they can connect. As with anyone, don't just send a request without identifying the connection."
~ Jennifer Chinn
www.linkedin.com/in/jenniferchinn/

"Build your professional network early and maintain a strong brand integrity."
~ Eyad (Ed) Batayeh, M.A.
www.linkedin.com/in/edbatayeh/

"When asking someone to join their network, be sure to include a personalized message!"
~ Jessica Knapik,
www.linkedin.com/in/jknapik/

"Become connected with everyone you meet!"
~ Sherry Yagiela, MBA
www.linkedin.com/in/sherryyagiela/

"Remember it is a professional network. Keep posts appropriate including profile picture. Paste from Word to ensure spelling is accurate."
~ Stephanie Maynard
www.linkedin.com/in/smmaynard/

16. **Look at your data and assess your progress.** The two data points I look at most often are the "Who Viewed Your Profile" trend line in my LinkedIn dashboard and my LinkedIn SSI. By periodically looking at these numbers, it helps me to keep focused on my progress.

As of the time I'm writing this, I've had 8,346 views of my profile in the past 90 days, and my LinkedIn SSI (www.mellermarketing.com/mylinkedinssi) is an 87.

Don't freak out if your numbers aren't as high. This is what I do for a living.

But also don't message me to gloat if your numbers are higher...

Who Viewed Your Profile - Trend Line
I always tell people when looking at your "Who Viewed Your Profile" trend line to focus on the PEAKS. That's when you were likely posting more often, interacting with others, or getting a lot of engagement on your posts. Do more of these activities.

Ignore the dips in your trend line. We all get them, but by focusing on the peaks, you will retrain your brain to focus on the activities that drive profile views.

Over time, I recommend that you focus on increasing and then maintaining your trend line.

If you have an optimized LinkedIn profile, you will be successful with your LinkedIn progress.

Remember: posts are for TELLING and your profile is for SELLING.

Your LinkedIn SSI

The LinkedIn Social Selling Index (SSI) is a feature offered by LinkedIn to measure your effectiveness at social selling. Keep in mind that LinkedIn wants you to upgrade to Sales Navigator, and that's part of the reason they offer all of us the ability to see our SSI score at any time, free.

Your LinkedIn Social Selling Index (SSI) is a score on a scale of 0 to 100 assigned by LinkedIn based on the activities and presence you have on LinkedIn. It essentially measures your ability to sell on LinkedIn, according to their magical formula.

It is an index, which means that 50 is average. It's like when I go to the pediatrician and they tell me that my child is in the 50th percentile for height or weight. They are average for the population of kids at my kid's age.

The highest I've been able to achieve for my SSI is an 87.

LinkedIn breaks this score into four categories, and you can read more about each category by viewing your results page. I recommend you use this index as one data point and even consider it as one benchmark. If you're not very active on LinkedIn, your score will be low: typically 20-24. As you increase your presence on LinkedIn, send more personalized invitations, engage (like, comment) on posts, and use the search function, your score will increase.

I have only met a few people with a score higher than 90, and these are typically people who are LinkedIn strategists who also have LinkedIn Sales Navigator. I have heard that you can't get above 90 unless you have Sales Navigator, and I personally would not pay to upgrade just to receive a higher score.

The goal is to use LinkedIn wisely to achieve your business goals, which may involve investing in LinkedIn Premium or LinkedIn Sales Navigator, but not always. At any rate, this is an interesting score to look up.

17. **Let LinkedIn notifications guide you.** Here are a few tips on how I use notifications.

Comments on posts that tag me (mention me). I reply with 5 or more words to thank them for the tag and to add a meaningful response. Sometimes, I include a question to keep the conversation going.

Work anniversaries. I reach out to congratulate the person on their timeline. However, I only do this if I know with 100% certainty that they still work at that company and they are still on this earth.

Live video notifications. If I have just five minutes to spare, I'll jump on the live video and add a quick comment. Or, I'll open the live video and say, "Hello from Metro Detroit." As I was writing this chapter, I did this on a live video by Ira Bowman. www.linkedin.com/in/ira-bowman

Trending now. LinkedIn offers articles that are trending. Jump on those links and add a comment or two or three. Just make sure that your comments include at least five words.

Promotions or new jobs. I recommend you click the link to go to the timeline where you can leave a five or more word comment of congratulations for the person and EVERYONE to see.

Those are just a few ways you can spend 15 minutes a day on LinkedIn to really ROCK on this platform.

Hi Brenda, let's connect! My favorite pie is pecan.
~ Susannah Waite
www.linkedin.com/in/susannahwaite

Chapter 38:

Concluding Remarks

Give everyone a chance to have a piece of the pie.
If the pie's not big enough, make a bigger pie.
~ *Dave Thomas*

Well, you did it! You completed reading the very first edition of Social Media Pie. At this point, you should be feeling much more knowledgeable about how to really use LinkedIn more effectively.

If you're feeling a bit overwhelmed, that's OK too. That means this book was chock full of useful tips and you now know there are opportunities for you on this amazing network.

It's kind of like pie on Thanksgiving. By the time we get to the dessert course, we are SO FULL that the pie – that we've been looking forward to ALL YEAR LONG – now feels so daunting and so overwhelming. But you know what? Take a small slice.

I remember my grandma at the holidays. She loved food. She used to make an AMAZING walnut torte that I still crave every Christmas. I can hear her voice at the end of Thanksgiving meal when the desserts (pies!) were brought onto the table.

"Oh, I'm so full. Just give me a little bit of each," she would say, and then giggle in her familiar, knowing laugh that made everyone smile.

Now, it's your turn to try a little bit of what I've taught you.

My hope for you at this point is that you have gained insights and perhaps even started to practice some of these techniques along the way.

My goal with each client session, each team training, and each conference presentation is that every person in the room learns something, and I hope you have learned a LOT from reading this book.

My dream is that every person who reads this book reaches out to me on LinkedIn and tags me in a post to share something they have learned.

ACTION ITEM: Want to have some fun and connect with fellow Social Media Pie book readers from across the world? Here's a quick exercise to do today…

Go onto LinkedIn and create a post NOW. Tell your network:

"I am just finishing a slice of #socialmediapiethebook by @Brenda-Meller (make sure you tag me!). My favorite pie is [tell us your favorite pie flavor].

One LinkedIn strategy I'm going to start using is [tell us one key takeaway].

Please comment below if you found this tip helpful."

Then, click on the #socialmediapiethebook hashtag to find other people who have posted using the hashtag, like their post, and leave a comment of five or more words. Then, invite them to connect with you on LinkedIn.

Be sure to include a personal note and mention your shared interest in #socialmediapiethebook when you connect.

By doing so, you are creating social media karma AND growing your LinkedIn network by connecting with amazing, like-minded people. YES, every person who reads my book is *amazing*.

Well, at least those following my advice and sharing it with others are.

The rest of you? I still believe in you, but you need to take the first step and DO something with this newfound knowledge. And THEN you will be amazing, too!

Those close to me know I've been talking about writing this book for years, and it's truly been a labor of love getting it into your hands.

Hopefully you smiled the first time you read the front of the book, or when you started flipping through its contents and found interesting tips right away.

Maybe you are one of the lucky ones I've mentioned in this book. If so, I'm honored to know you and I thank you for helping to provide me with content to fill these pages. Maybe you should buy a copy (or two, or ten) and join me at a book signing sometime? We'll talk about that later.

As for the rest of you, go forth and make me proud. I don't know about you, but I'm going to go celebrate with a slice of my favorite pie!

Oh...and my favorite pie is Pecan. I think it is a favorite because it reminds me of Thanksgiving celebrations where love and gratitude were everywhere. It was an anticipated homemade treat that always made a sweet ending to a perfect day!
~ Cynthia Brawley
www.linkedin.com/in/brawleycopywritingagency

Acknowledgements

When I finally decided to write a book about LinkedIn, I knew that it would take a commitment on my part but also the support of my friends, family, connections, and LinkedIn community to get this done.

I have a LOT of people to thank. So here it goes.

First, I have to thank Erika Crocker (www.linkedin.com/in/erika-crocker-moises-1372a54), who convinced me back in 2006 to join this growing professional networking site. I will always fondly recall working with Erika and her love of Starbucks. Every morning, she'd bring in a venti iced coffee and a venti hot coffee; her energy level never wavered!

Second, thank you John Lichtenberg (www.linkedin.com/in/lichtenberg) who was recruiting for a marketing manager in 2008 and responded to my InMail message (still the best $29.99 I ever paid on LinkedIn). John said mine was the first resume he received on LinkedIn alone, with at least 300 applicants on LinkedIn, and hundreds more through HR, Monster, HotJobs, etc. If it weren't for LinkedIn and my using it to approach the job search differently, you wouldn't be reading this today. We had a blast working together. I recall John had a sign in his office that read, "If you're not making at least 9 mistakes a week, you're not trying hard enough." That always made me feel good when walking into his office after making a mistake!

I want to thank all of my fellow Toastmasters members. I joined this public speaking group back in 2007 hoping to improve my speaking skills. One of my first speech topics was to tell people about LinkedIn. I recall fellow Toastmaster member Jim McVicar (www.linkedin.com/in/mcvicar) giving me feedback, helping me to gain confidence in my speech.

To my favorite grade school teacher of all time, Bonnie Baranowski (www. linkedin.com/in/bonnie-baranowski-7782b270). She instilled in me a love of reading and writing. I remember winning the spelling bee when I was in her fifth-grade class at L'Anse Creuse Elementary School, Marie C. Graham in Harrison Township, Michigan. I can still picture her standing over me, beaming in pride in class. I am friends with her on Facebook and try to acknowledge her on National Teachers' Day each year.

Thank you to David Bradley (www.linkedin.com/in/david-bradley-681 83767) for inviting me to be a speaker at Oakland Community College's 'Lunch and Learn' event in May 2019. One of your attendees was instrumental in connecting me with someone who helped me get this book off the ground.

Thank you to Michael Dwyer (www.linkedin.com/in/rochesterwriters) for inviting me to speak at your Rochester Writers' Annual Fall Conference and present, "LinkedIn for Authors," to a room full of current authors, aspiring authors, and fellow speakers, including Don Staley.

Thank you, Don Staley (www.linkedin.com/in/donstaley) for attending my LinkedIn presentation at the Rochester Writers' Conference and for writing your book, "How to Write a Book in 30 Days," which I bought after chatting with you in the lobby after my talk that day. I proceeded to read your book over the next week; I started writing the day after finishing it. You gave me the momentum I needed to actually BEGIN the writing process.

Thank you to my mom, Sandy Zawacki, who instilled in me a love of reading at a very young age. I remember her taking me and my sisters to the library to pick out as many books as we wanted when we were little. My love of reading has continued throughout my life, and this book is dedicated in part to her memory. My love of pie is due in part to my mom, too. More on that later.

Thank you to my sister, Lisa Piotrowski and to my dad, Michael Zawacki (neither are on LinkedIn) for supporting me while I pursued my graduate degree. I didn't know it at the time, but this prepared me for the rigor and gave me the drive required to continue writing at all hours of the night to finish my book. You both helped me with the kids while I was pursuing my degree and I'll forever be grateful.

Thank you to all my fellow Meller Marketing #LinkedInROCKSTARS for inspiring me, for educating me, for supporting me, and for sharing your love of LinkedIn with me. As of this publishing, I have 70 names on the LinkedIn trainer version of this list, including (in alphabetical order by first name):

Adrian Herzkovich (www.linkedin.com/in/adrianherzkovich)
Adrienne Tom (www.linkedin.com/in/adriennetom)
Ana Lokotkova (www.linkedin.com/in/alokotkova)
Andy Foote (www.linkedin.com/in/andyfoote)
Angus Grady (www.linkedin.com/in/angusgrady)
Anne Pryor (www.linkedin.com/in/annepryor)
Baschi Sale (www.linkedin.com/in/baschi)
Beth Granger (www.linkedin.com/in/bethgranger)
Bobby Umar (www.linkedin.com/in/bobbyumar)
Brenda Meller (Me) (www.linkedin.com/in/brendameller)
Brynne Tillman (www.linkedin.com/in/brynnetillman)
Charlie Whyman (www.linkedin.com/in/charliewhyman)

Cher Jones (www.linkedin.com/in/itscherjones)
Chrissie Zavicar (www.linkedin.com/in/chrissiezavicar)
Craig Wasilchak (www.linkedin.com/in/craigwasilchak)
Crystal Thies (www.linkedin.com/in/crystalthies)
David Petherick (www.linkedin.com/in/davidpetherick)
Dean Seddon (www.linkedin.com/in/deanseddoncom)
Debbie Wemyss (www.linkedin.com/in/debbiewemyss)
Debra Mathias (www.linkedin.com/in/debramathias)
Dennis Brown (www.linkedin.com/in/askdennisbrown)
Derick Mildred (www.linkedin.com/in/results-formula)
Diane Darling (www.linkedin.com/in/dianedarling)
Donna Serdula (www.linkedin.com/in/todonna)
Elisa B. Bennett (www.linkedin.com/in/elisabbennett)
Erin Kennedy (www.linkedin.com/in/erinkennedycprw)
Fabio Marrama (www.linkedin.com/in/fabiomarrama)
Greg Cooper (www.linkedin.com/in/gregcoopers)
Guy Strijbosch (www.linkedin.com/in/guystrijbosch)
Helen Pritchard (www.linkedin.com/in/helenpritchard)
Jason Boone (www.linkedin.com/in/jasonmboone)
Jeff Young (www.linkedin.com/in/jeffyoungralemoi)
Jennifer Corcoran (www.linkedin.com/in/jennifercorcoran1)
Jess Tiffany (www.linkedin.com/in/jesstiffany)
Jessica Hernandez (www.linkedin.com/in/jessicaholbrook)
Jessica Jones (www.linkedin.com/in/askjessicajones)
Jillian Bullock (www.linkedin.com/in/jillianbullock)
Jo Saunders (www.linkedin.com/in/josaunders)
Joe Apfelbaum (www.linkedin.com/in/joeapfelbaum)
John Espirian (www.linkedin.com/in/johnespirian)
Judi Hays (www.linkedin.com/in/judihays)
Kenneth Lang (www.linkedin.com/in/langk)
Kevin Turner (www.linkedin.com/in/president)
Kotryna Kurt (www.linkedin.com/in/kotryna-kurt)
Kylie Chown (www.linkedin.com/in/kylie-chown-training-brisbane)
Lynnaire Johnston (www.linkedin.com/in/lynnairejohnston)

Lynne Williams (www.linkedin.com/in/lynnewilliams)
Madeline Mann (www.linkedin.com/in/madelinemann)
Marc Halpert (www.linkedin.com/in/marchalpert)
Mark Stonham (www.linkedin.com/in/markstonham)
Melanie Goodman (www.linkedin.com/in/melaniegoodmanfinan cialmarketing)
Mic Adam (www.linkedin.com/in/micadam)
Miles Duncan (www.linkedin.com/in/milesduncan)
Nigel Cliffe (www.linkedin.com/in/nigeljcliffe)
Petra Fisher (www.linkedin.com/in/petrafisher)
Phil Gerbyshak (www.linkedin.com/in/philgerb)
Rhonda Sher (www.linkedin.com/in/rhondalsher)
Richard van der Blom (www.linkedin.com/in/richardvanderblom)
Sam Rathling (www.linkedin.com/in/samrathling-linkedinexpert)
Sandra Long (www.linkedin.com/in/longsandra)
Shelly Elsliger (www.linkedin.com/in/selsliger)
Sid Clark (www.linkedin.com/in/sidclark)
Stella Da Silva (www.linkedin.com/in/stellalicious)
Steve Phillip (www.linkedin.com/in/stevephillipsalestrainer)
Susan P Joyce (www.linkedin.com/in/susanjoyce)
Teddy Burriss (www.linkedin.com/in/tlburriss)
Terry Bean (www.linkedin.com/in/terrybean)
Tony Restell (www.linkedin.com/in/tonyrestell)
Vic Williams (www.linkedin.com/in/ professional-speaker-vic-williams-changeleadership)
Victoria Ipri (www.linkedin.com/in/victoriaipri)
Wayne Breitbarth (www.linkedin.com/in/waynebreitbarth)

And a special shout-out to two of the above LinkedIn rockstars in particular:

John Espirian (www.linkedin.com/in/johnespirian), who was one of the first people I saw who analyzed his own LinkedIn data. He inspired me to start tracking my own data, which led me to make and publish the

Rockstar list, propelling my LinkedIn consulting business, eventually inspiring me to write this book. John's book, "Content DNA" also encouraged me as I began writing. His book is a great read for any marketer or individual seeking insight into more powerful online communication methods, including content marketing, social media marketing, and more.

Also, Jeff Young (www.linkedin.com/in/jeffyoungralemoi) who created an acronym for the word "ROCKSTAR" to perfectly describe the type of LinkedIn trainer I aspire to be, and the type of person who makes my list:

"If you want to really get involved, build a network and make a difference on LinkedIn, then be a R-O-C-K-S-T-A-R like this folks:

Real desire to help
Outstanding knowledge
Caring attitude
Kind and giving
Super connections
Trust your network
Actively engage
Relationship builder"

To my children, Joshua and Charlotte, thank you for supporting me as I attempted to write at least one hour every day for a month. You are both my inspiration and my joy, even when we don't eat dinner until 8 p.m. on a Sunday night because I'm doing client work. I'm hoping both of you will be asked to sign autographs at my book signing party and pass out pie to celebrate. Yes, Joshua. You *have* to go. And, no, Charlotte you can't stay home with Daddy. He'll be there, too.

To my husband, Chris (www.linkedin.com/in/chrismeller67), thank you for your support at every stage of my career. Thank you for never doubting me for a second when I decided to leave corporate and stay on my own. Thanks for all you do to help share duties around the house so that I could find the time to fit in a major project like writing a book. And thank you most of all for your love and for making me drinks on 'Martini Friday' while I was writing my book. You are pretty awesome and I'm glad I married you.

Thank you to all my extended family, friends, supporters, followers, and fans, and, of course, to my amazing LinkedIn community. As of this writing, I have 16,618 LinkedIn connections and 50,385 followers. If it wasn't for each of you, I wouldn't be writing this book.

I've heard from many people over the years that the guidance and tips I've provided have been helpful in your careers, in your job searches, in your business launches, in your companies, and in your professional networks. When I thought about writing a book, many of you encouraged me along.

While I've shared a lot of this knowledge with you in different places (on LinkedIn, on YouTube, in blogs, etc.), I'm hoping you'll find this book to be a great resource for you in your LinkedIn journey. Who knows? Maybe you'll be the next person in the audience to win a pie from me!

Whether you've been given a copy of this book, bought this book (thank you!), or received this book as a gift or on loan from the library or from a friend, I hope you will enjoy reading this as much as I love pie.

ABOUT THE AUTHOR

For the past ten years, Brenda has been embracing social media to help propel her personal and professional efforts and now through Meller Marketing, she helps people and businesses with marketing and social media, specializing in LinkedIn.

She first realized the power of social media when making a career change using LinkedIn at the height of Michigan's downturn in 2008. She started sharing her knowledge of social media through workshops, webinars, presentations, and via blogs.

In 2017, her side hustle led to her dream job with the launch of Meller Marketing. In 2019, she set and met a personal stretch goal and rewarded herself with a promotion to Chief Engagement Officer.

Brenda's approach has always been to present information in a "judgement-free" zone, where there are no bad questions, and to make sure every attendee gains new insights that can be put to use right away.

In addition to being self-taught across social media channels (LinkedIn, Facebook, Twitter, Instagram, Pinterest, YouTube, Glassdoor, and more), Brenda has a solid marketing education. She earned a bachelor of science in business administration degree with a specialization in marketing communications from Central Michigan University in Mt. Pleasant, Michigan, and a dual MBA and master of science in marketing from Walsh College. She also earned her competent communicator (CC) and competent leader (CL) status in Toastmasters International, a public speaking organization.

MichBusiness named Brenda a MichBusiness Most Valuable Professional in 2017 and a Marketing & PR Prophet for Meller Marketing in 2019. Meller Marketing was also named a 2019 HRUnite! Advocate, celebrating her support of the HR community.

She is a member of Inforum, Michigan's largest professional women's networking association, where she also leads the Troy networking group. She is also a member and serves on the board of Detroit Together Digital. Meller Marketing is a member of the Troy Chamber of Commerce, the Detroit Economic Club, and the Sterling Heights Regional Chamber.

Brenda is an enthusiastic speaker who loves engaging with audiences, both at conferences and corporate events. In 2019, she became a national speaker.

You can find Brenda Meller and Meller Marketing online on all the major social media channels.

Other Important Facts: Brenda loves coffee, chocolate, and pie. In her downtime, she enjoys jigsaw puzzles.

INDEX

C

Printed in Great Britain
by Amazon